POEMS

IN TWO VOLUMES

POEMS
IN TWO VOLUMES

BY WILLIAM WORDSWORTH

1807

UNITED KINGDOM

CONTENTS

POEMS IN TWO VOLUMES,

VOL. I.

BY WILLIAM WORDSWORTH

AUTHOR OF *THE LYRICAL BALLADS.*

TO THE DAISY.

In youth from rock to rock I went
From hill to hill, in discontent
Of pleasure high and turbulent,
 Most pleas'd when most uneasy;
But now my own delights I make,
My thirst at every rill can slake,
And gladly Nature's love partake
 Of thee, sweet Daisy!

 When soothed a while by milder airs,
Thee Winter in the garland wears 10
That thinly shades his few grey hairs;
 Spring cannot shun thee;
Whole summer fields are thine by right;
And Autumn, melancholy Wight!
Doth in thy crimson head delight
 When rains are on thee.

In shoals and bands, a morrice train,
Thou greet'st the Traveller in the lane;
If welcome once thou count'st it gain;
　　Thou art not daunted, 20
Nor car'st if thou be set at naught;
And oft alone in nooks remote
We meet thee, like a pleasant thought,
　　When such are wanted.

　　Be Violets in their secret mews
The flowers the wanton Zephyrs chuse;
Proud be the Rose, with rains and dews
　　Her head impearling;
Thou liv'st with less ambitious aim,
Yet hast not gone without thy fame; 30
Thou art indeed by many a claim
　　The Poet's darling.

　　If to a rock from rains he fly,
Or, some bright day of April sky,
Imprison'd by hot sunshine lie
　　Near the green holly,
And wearily at length should fare;
He need but look about, and there
Thou art! a Friend at hand, to scare
　　His melancholy. 40

　　A hundred times, by rock or bower,
Ere thus I have lain couch'd an hour,
Have I derived from thy sweet power
　　Some apprehension;
Some steady love; some brief delight;
Some memory that had taken flight;

Some chime of fancy wrong or right;
    Or stray invention.

If stately passions in me burn,
And one chance look to Thee should turn, 50
I drink out of an humbler urn
    A lowlier pleasure;
The homely sympathy that heeds
The common life, our nature breeds;
A wisdom fitted to the needs
    Of hearts at leisure.

When, smitten by the morning ray,
I see thee rise alert and gay,
Then, chearful Flower! my spirits play
    With kindred motion: 60
At dusk, I've seldom mark'd thee press
The ground, as if in thankfulness,
Without some feeling, more or less,
    Of true devotion.

And all day long I number yet,
All seasons through, another debt,
Which I wherever thou art met,
    To thee am owing;
An instinct call it, a blind sense;
A happy, genial influence, 70
Coming one knows not how nor whence,
    Nor whither going.

Child of the Year! that round dost run
Thy course, bold lover of the sun,
And chearful when the day's begun

As morning Leveret,
Thou long the Poet's praise shalt gain;
Thou wilt be more belov'd by men
In times to come; thou not in vain
Art Nature's Favorite. 80

LOUISA.

* * * * *

I met Louisa in the shade;
And, having seen that lovely Maid,
Why should I fear to say
That she is ruddy, fleet, and strong;
And down the rocks can leap along,
Like rivulets in May?

And she hath smiles to earth unknown;
Smiles, that with motion of their own
Do spread, and sink, and rise;
That come and go with endless play, 10
And ever, as they pass away,
Are hidden in her eyes.

She loves her fire, her Cottage-home;
Yet o'er the moorland will she roam
In weather rough and bleak;
And when against the wind she strains,
Oh! might I kiss the mountain rains
That sparkle on her cheek.

Take all that's mine 'beneath the moon',
If I with her but half a noon 20
May sit beneath the walls
Of some old cave, or mossy nook,
When up she winds along the brook,
To hunt the waterfalls.

FIDELITY.

* * * * *

A barking sound the Shepherd hears,
A cry as of a Dog or Fox;
He halts, and searches with his eyes
Among the scatter'd rocks:
And now at distance can discern
A stirring in a brake of fern;
From which immediately leaps out
A Dog, and yelping runs about.

The Dog is not of mountain breed;
It's motions, too, are wild and shy; 10
With something, as the Shepherd thinks,
Unusual in its' cry:
Nor is there any one in sight
All round, in Hollow or on Height;
Nor shout, nor whistle strikes his ear;
What is the Creature doing here?

It was a Cove, a huge Recess,
That keeps till June December's snow;
A lofty Precipice in front,
A silent Tarn [1] below! 20
Far in the bosom of Helvellyn,
Remote from public Road or Dwelling,
Pathway, or cultivated land;
From trace of human foot or hand.

[Footnote 1: A Tarn is a small Mere or Lake mostly high up in the
mountains.]

There, sometimes does a leaping Fish
Send through the Tarn a lonely chear;
The Crags repeat the Raven's croak,
In symphony austere;
Thither the Rainbow comes, the Cloud;
And Mists that spread the flying shroud; 30
And Sun-beams; and the sounding blast,
That, if it could, would hurry past,
But that enormous Barrier binds it fast.

Not knowing what to think, a while
The Shepherd stood: then makes his way
Towards the Dog, o'er rocks and stones,
As quickly as he may;
Nor far had gone before he found
A human skeleton on the ground,
Sad sight! the Shepherd with a sigh 40
Looks round, to learn the history.

From those abrupt and perilous rocks,
The Man had fallen, that place of fear!

At length upon the Shepherd's mind
It breaks, and all is clear:
He instantly recall'd the Name,
And who he was, and whence he came;
Remember'd, too, the very day
On which the Traveller pass'd this way.

But hear a wonder now, for sake 50
Of which this mournful Tale I tell!
A lasting monument of words
This wonder merits well.
The Dog, which still was hovering nigh,
Repeating the same timid cry,
This Dog had been through three months' space
A Dweller in that savage place.

Yes, proof was plain that since the day
On which the Traveller thus had died
The Dog had watch'd about the spot, 60
Or by his Master's side:
How nourish'd here through such long time
He knows, who gave that love sublime,
And gave that strength of feeling, great
Above all human estimate.

SHE WAS A PHANTOM OF DELIGHT

* * * * *

She was a Phantom of delight
When first she gleam'd upon my sight;
A lovely Apparition, sent
To be a moment's ornament;
Her eyes as stars of Twilight fair;
Like Twilight's, too, her dusky hair;
But all things else about her drawn
From May-time and the chearful Dawn;
A dancing Shape, an Image gay,
To haunt, to startle, and way-lay. 10

I saw her upon nearer view,
A Spirit, yet a Woman too!
Her household motions light and free,
And steps of virgin liberty;
A countenance in which did meet
Sweet records, promises as sweet;
A Creature not too bright or good
For human nature's daily food;
For transient sorrows, simple wiles,
Praise, blame, love, kisses, tears, and smiles. 20

And now I see with eye serene
The very pulse of the machine;
A Being breathing thoughtful breath;
A Traveller betwixt life and death;
The reason firm, the temperate will,
Endurance, foresight, strength and skill;
A perfect Woman; nobly plann'd,

To warn, to comfort, and command;
And yet a Spirit still, and bright
With something of an angel light. 30

THE REDBREAST AND THE BUTTERFLY.

Art thou the Bird whom Man loves best,
The pious Bird with the scarlet breast,
   Our little English Robin;
The Bird that comes about our doors
When Autumn winds are sobbing?
Art thou the Peter of Norway Boors?
   Their Thomas in Finland,
   And Russia far inland?
The Bird, whom by some name or other
All men who know thee call their Brother, 10
The Darling of Children and men?
Could Father Adam open his eyes,
And see this sight beneath the skies,
He'd wish to close them again.

If the Butterfly knew but his friend
Hither his flight he would bend,
And find his way to me
Under the branches of the tree:
In and out, he darts about;
His little heart is throbbing: 20
Can this be the Bird, to man so good,
   Our consecrated Robin!

That, after their bewildering,
Did cover with leaves the little children,
   So painfully in the wood?

   What ail'd thee Robin that thou could'st pursue
   A beautiful Creature,
That is gentle by nature?
Beneath the summer sky
From flower to flower let him fly; 30
'Tis all that he wishes to do.

   The Chearer Thou of our in-door sadness,
He is the Friend of our summer gladness:
What hinders, then, that ye should be
Playmates in the sunny weather,
And fly about in the air together?
Like the hues of thy breast
His beautiful wings in crimson are drest,
A brother he seems of thine own:
If thou would'st be happy in thy nest, 40
O pious Bird! whom Man loves best,
Love him, or leave him alone!

THE SAILOR'S MOTHER.

* * * * *

   One morning (raw it was and wet,
   A foggy day in winter time)
   A Woman in the road I met,

Not old, though something past her prime:
Majestic in her person, tall and straight;
And like a Roman matron's was her mien and gait.

The ancient Spirit is not dead;
Old times, thought I, are breathing there;
Proud was I that my country bred
Such strength, a dignity so fair: 10
She begg'd an alms, like one in poor estate;
I look'd at her again, nor did my pride abate.

When from these lofty thoughts I woke,
With the first word I had to spare
I said to her, "Beneath your Cloak
What's that which on your arm you bear?"
She answer'd soon as she the question heard,
"A simple burthen, Sir, a little Singing-bird."

And, thus continuing, she said,
"I had a Son, who many a day 20
Sail'd on the seas; but he is dead;
In Denmark he was cast away;
And I have been as far as Hull, to see
What clothes he might have left, or other property."

"The Bird and Cage they both were his;
'Twas my Son's Bird; and neat and trim
He kept it: many voyages
This Singing-bird hath gone with him;
When last he sail'd he left the Bird behind;
As it might be, perhaps, from bodings of his mind." 30

"He to a Fellow-lodger's care
Had left it, to be watch'd and fed,
Till he came back again; and there
I found it when my Son was dead;
And now, God help me for my little wit!
I trail it with me, Sir! he took so much delight in it."

TO THE SMALL CELANDINE

[footnote: common pilewort.]
* * * * *

Pansies, Lilies, Kingcups, Daisies,
Let them live upon their praises;
Long as there's a sun that sets
Primroses will have their glory;
Long as there are Violets,
They will have a place in story:
There's a flower that shall be mine,
'Tis the little Celandine.

Eyes of some men travel far
For the finding of a star; 10
Up and down the heavens they go,
Men that keep a mighty rout!
I'm as great as they, I trow,
Since the day I found thee out,
Little flower!—I'll make a stir
Like a great Astronomer.

Modest, yet withal an Elf
Bold, and lavish of thyself,
Since we needs must first have met
I have seen thee, high and low, 20
Thirty years or more, and yet
'Twas a face I did not know;
Thou hast now, go where I may,
Fifty greetings in a day.

Ere a leaf is on a bush,
In the time before the Thrush
Has a thought about its nest,
Thou wilt come with half a call,
Spreading out thy glossy breast
Like a careless Prodigal; 30
Telling tales about the sun,
When we've little warmth, or none.

Poets, vain men in their mood!
Travel with the multitude;
Never heed them; I aver
That they all are wanton Wooers;
But the thrifty Cottager,
Who stirs little out of doors,
Joys to spy thee near her home,
Spring is coming, Thou art come! 40

Comfort have thou of thy merit,
Kindly, unassuming Spirit!
Careless of thy neighbourhood,
Thou dost shew thy pleasant face
On the moor, and in the wood.

In the lane—there's not a place,
Howsoever mean it be,
But 'tis good enough for thee.

Ill befal the yellow Flowers,
Children of the flaring hours! 50
Buttercups, that will be seen,
Whether we will see or no;
Others, too, of lofty mien;
They have done as worldlings do,
Taken praise that should be thine,
Little, humble Celandine!

Prophet of delight and mirth,
Scorn'd and slighted upon earth!
Herald of a mighty band,
Of a joyous train ensuing, 60
Singing at my heart's command,
In the lanes my thoughts pursuing,
I will sing, as doth behove,
Hymns in praise of what I love!

TO THE SAME FLOWER.

Pleasures newly found are sweet
When they lie about our feet:
February last my heart
First at sight of thee was glad;
All unheard of as thou art,
Thou must needs, I think, have had,

Celandine! and long ago,
Praise of which I nothing know.

I have not a doubt but he,
Whosoe'er the man might be, 10
Who the first with pointed rays,
(Workman worthy to be sainted)
Set the Sign-board in a blaze,
When the risen sun he painted,
Took the fancy from a glance
At thy glittering countenance.

Soon as gentle breezes bring
News of winter's vanishing,
And the children build their bowers,
Sticking 'kerchief-plots of mold 20
All about with full-blown flowers,
Thick as sheep in shepherd's fold!
With the proudest Thou art there,
Mantling in the tiny square.

Often have I sigh'd to measure
By myself a lonely pleasure;
Sigh'd to think, I read a book
Only read perhaps by me;
Yet I long could overlook
Thy bright coronet and Thee, 30
And thy arch and wily ways,
And thy store of other praise.

Blithe of heart, from week to week
Thou dost play at hide-and-seek;
While the patient Primrose sits

Like a Beggar in the cold,
Thou, a Flower of wiser wits,
Slipp'st into thy shelter'd hold:
Bright as any of the train
When ye all are out again. 40

   Thou art not beyond the moon,
But a thing "beneath our shoon;"
Let, as old Magellen did,
Others roam about the sea;
Build who will a pyramid;
Praise it is enough for me,
If there be but three or four
Who will love my little Flower.

CHARACTER OF THE HAPPY WARRIOR.

   Who is the happy Warrior? Who is he
Whom every Man in arms should wish to be?
—It is the generous Spirit, who, when brought
Among the tasks of real life, hath wrought
Upon the plan that pleased his childish thought:
Whose high endeavours are an inward light
That make the path before him always bright:
Who, with a natural instinct to discern
What knowledge can perform, is diligent to learn;
Abides by this resolve, and stops not there, 10
But makes his moral being his prime care;
Who, doom'd to go in company with Pain,

And Fear, and Bloodshed, miserable train!
Turns his necessity to glorious gain;
In face of these doth exercise a power
Which is our human-nature's highest dower;
Controls them and subdues, transmutes, bereaves
Of their bad influence, and their good receives;
By objects, which might force the soul to abate
Her feeling, render'd more compassionate; 20
Is placable because occasions rise
So often that demand such sacrifice;
More skilful in self-knowledge, even more pure,
As tempted more; more able to endure,
As more expos'd to suffering and distress;
Thence, also, more alive to tenderness.
Tis he whose law is reason; who depends
Upon that law as on the best of friends;
Whence, in a state where men are tempted still
To evil for a guard against worse ill, 30
And what in quality or act is best
Doth seldom on a right foundation rest,
He fixes good on good alone, and owes
To virtue every triumph that he knows:
—Who, if he rise to station of command,
Rises by open means; and there will stand
On honourable terms, or else retire,
And in himself possess his own desire;
Who comprehends his trust, and to the same
Keeps faithful with a singleness of aim; 40
And therefore does not stoop, nor lie in wait
For wealth, or honors, or for worldly state;
Whom they must follow; on whose head must fall,

Like showers of manna, if they come at all:
Whose powers shed round him in the common strife,
Or mild concerns of ordinary life,
A constant influence, a peculiar grace;
But who, if he be called upon to face
Some awful moment to which heaven has join'd
Great issues, good or bad for human-kind, 50
Is happy as a Lover; and attired
With sudden brightness like a Man inspired;
And through the heat of conflict keeps the law
In calmness made, and sees what he foresaw;
Or if an unexpected call succeed,
Come when it will, is equal to the need:
—He who, though thus endued as with a sense
And faculty for storm and turbulence,
Is yet a Soul whose master bias leans
To home-felt pleasures and to gentle scenes; 60
Sweet images! which, wheresoe'er he be,
Are at his heart; and such fidelity
It is his darling passion to approve;
More brave for this, that he hath much to love:
'Tis, finally, the Man, who, lifted high,
Conspicuous object in a Nation's eye,
Or left unthought-of in obscurity,
Who, with a toward or untoward lot,
Prosperous or adverse, to his wish or not,
Plays, in the many games of life, that one 70
Where what he most doth value must be won;
Whom neither shape of danger can dismay,
Nor thought of tender happiness betray;
Who, not content that former worth stand fast,
Looks forward, persevering to the last,

From well to better, daily self-surpast:
Who, whether praise of him must walk the earth
For ever, and to noble deeds give birth,
Or He must go to dust without his fame,
And leave a dead unprofitable name, 80
Finds comfort in himself and in his cause;
And, while the mortal mist is gathering, draws
His breath in confidence of Heaven's applause;
This is the happy Warrior; this is He
Whom every Man in arms should wish to be.

* * * * *

*The above Verses mere written soon after tidings had been received of
the Death of Lord Nelson, which event directed the Author's thoughts
to the subject. His respect for the memory of his great fellow-countryman
induces him to mention this; though he is well aware that the Verses
must suffer from any connection in the Reader's mind with a Name so
illustrious.*

THE HORN OF EGREMONT CASTLE.

When the Brothers reach'd the gateway,
Eustace pointed with his lance
To the Horn which there was hanging;
Horn of the inheritance.
Horn it was which none could sound,
No one upon living ground,

Save He who came as rightful Heir
To Egremont's Domains and Castle fair.

Heirs from ages without record
Had the House of Lucie born, 10
Who of right had claim'd the Lordship
By the proof upon the Horn:
Each at the appointed hour
Tried the Horn, it own'd his power;
He was acknowledged: and the blast
Which good Sir Eustace sounded was the last.

With his lance Sir Eustace pointed,
And to Hubert thus said he,
"What I speak this Horn shall witness
For thy better memory. 20
Hear, then, and neglect me not!
At this time, and on this spot,
The words are utter'd from my heart,
As my last earnest prayer ere we depart."

"On good service we are going
Life to risk by sea and land;
In which course if Christ our Saviour
Do my sinful soul demand,
Hither come thou back straightway,
Hubert, if alive that day; 30
Return, and sound the Horn, that we
May have a living House still left in thee!"

"Fear not," quickly answer'd Hubert;
"As I am thy Father's son,
What thou askest, noble Brother,

With God's favour shall be done."
So were both right well content:
From the Castle forth they went.
And at the head of their Array
To Palestine the Brothers took their way. 40

    Side by side they fought (the Lucies
Were a line for valour fam'd)
And where'er their strokes alighted
There the Saracens were tam'd.
Whence, then, could it come the thought,
By what evil spirit brought?
Oh! can a brave Man wish to take
His Brother's life, for Land's and Castle's sake?

    "Sir!" the Ruffians said to Hubert,
"Deep he lies in Jordan flood."— 50
Stricken by this ill assurance,
Pale and trembling Hubert stood.
"Take your earnings."—Oh! that I
Could have seen my Brother die!
It was a pang that vex'd him then;
And oft returned, again, and yet again.

    Months pass'd on, and no Sir Eustace!
Nor of him were tidings heard.
Wherefore, bold as day, the Murderer
Back again to England steer'd. 60
To his Castle Hubert sped;
He has nothing now to dread.
But silent and by stealth he came,
And at an hour which nobody could name.

None could tell if it were night-time,
Night or day, at even or morn;
For the sound was heard by no one
Of the proclamation-horn.
But bold Hubert lives in glee:
Months and years went smilingly; 70
With plenty was his table spread;
And bright the Lady is who shares his bed.

Likewise he had Sons and Daughters;
And, as good men do, he sate
At his board by these surrounded,
Flourishing in fair estate.
And, while thus in open day
Once he sate, as old books say,
A blast was utter'd from the Horn,
Where by the Castle-gate it hung forlorn. 80

'Tis the breath of good Sir Eustace!
He is come to claim his right:
Ancient Castle, Woods, and Mountains
Hear the challenge with delight.
Hubert! though the blast be blown
He is helpless and alone:
Thou hast a dungeon, speak the word!
And there he may be lodg'd, and thou be Lord.

Speak! astounded Hubert cannot;
And if power to speak he had, 90
All are daunted, all the household
Smitten to the heart, and sad.
'Tis Sir Eustace; if it be
Living Man, it must be he!

Thus Hubert thought in his dismay,
And by a Postern-gate he slunk away.

   Long, and long was he unheard of:
To his Brother then he came,
Made confession, ask'd forgiveness,
Ask'd it by a Brother's name, 100
And by all the saints in heaven;
And of Eustace was forgiv'n:
Then in a Convent went to hide
His melancholy head, and there he died.

   But Sir Eustace, whom good Angels
Had preserv'd from Murderers' hands,
And from Pagan chains had rescued,
Liv'd with honour on his lands.
Sons he had, saw Sons of theirs:
And through ages, Heirs of Heirs, 110
A long posterity renown'd,
Sounded the Horn which they alone could sound.

THE AFFLICTION OF MARGARET —— OF ——

* * * * *

   Where art thou, my beloved Son,
Where art thou, worse to me than dead?
Oh find me prosperous or undone!
Or, if the grave be now thy bed,
Why am I ignorant of the same

That I may rest; and neither blame,
Nor sorrow may attend thy name?

Seven years, alas, to have received
No tidings of an only child;
To have despair'd, and have believ'd, 10
And be for evermore beguil'd;
Sometimes with thoughts of very bliss!
I catch at them, and then I miss;
Was ever darkness like to this?

He was among the prime in worth,
An object beauteous to behold;
Well born, well bred; I sent him forth
Ingenuous, innocent, and bold:
If things ensued that wanted grace,
As hath been said, they were not base; 20
And never blush was on my face.

Ah! little doth the Young One dream,
When full of play and childish cares,
What power hath even his wildest scream,
Heard by his Mother unawares!
He knows it not, he cannot guess:
Years to a Mother bring distress;
But do not make her love the less.

Neglect me! no I suffer'd long
From that ill thought; and being blind, 30
Said, "Pride shall help me in my wrong;
Kind mother have I been, as kind
As ever breathed:" and that is true;

I've wet my path with tears like dew,
Weeping for him when no one knew.

My Son, if thou be humbled, poor,
Hopeless of honour and of gain,
Oh! do not dread thy mother's door;
Think not of me with grief and pain:
I now can see with better eyes; 40
And worldly grandeur I despise,
And fortune with her gifts and lies

Alas! the fowls of Heaven have wings,
And blasts of Heaven will aid their flight;
They mount, how short a voyage brings
The Wanderers back to their delight!
Chains tie us down by land and sea;
And wishes, vain as mine, may be
All that is left to comfort thee.

Perhaps some dungeon hears thee groan, 50
Maim'd, mangled by inhuman men;
Or thou upon a Desart thrown
Inheritest the Lion's Den;
Or hast been summoned to the Deep,
Thou, Thou and all thy mates, to keep
An incommunicable sleep.

I look for Ghosts; but none will force
Their way to me; 'tis falsely said
That there was ever intercourse
Betwixt the living and the dead; 60
For, surely, then I should have sight

Of Him I wait for day and night,
With love and longings infinite.

My apprehensions come in crowds;
I dread the rustling of the grass;
The very shadows of the clouds
Have power to shake me as they pass:
I question things, and do not find
One that will answer to my mind;
And all the world appears unkind. 70

Beyond participation lie
My troubles, and beyond relief:
If any chance to heave a sigh
They pity me, and not my grief.
Then come to me, my Son, or send
Some tidings that my woes may end;
I have no other earthly friend.

THE KITTEN AND THE FALLING LEAVES.

* * * * *

That way look, my Infant, lo!
What a pretty baby show!
See the Kitten on the Wall,
Sporting with the leaves that fall,
Wither'd leaves, one, two, and three,
From the lofty Elder-tree!

Through the calm and frosty air
Of this morning bright and fair,
Eddying round and round they sink
Softly, slowly: one might think, 10
From the motions that are made,
Every little leaf convey'd
Sylph or Faery hither tending,
To this lower world descending,
Each invisible and mute,
In his wavering parachute.
—But the Kitten, how she starts,
Crouches, stretches, paws, and darts;
First at one and then its fellow
Just as light and just as yellow; 20
There are many now—now one—
Now they stop; and there are none—
What intenseness of desire
In her upward eye of fire!
With a tiger-leap half way
Now she meets the coming prey,
Lets it go as fast, and then
Has it in her power again:
Now she works with three or four,
Like an Indian Conjuror; 30
Quick as he in feats of art,
Far beyond in joy of heart.
Were her antics play'd in the eye
Of a thousand Standers-by,
Clapping hands with shout and stare,
What would little Tabby care
For the plaudits of the Crowd?

Over happy to be proud,
Over wealthy in the treasure
Of her own exceeding pleasure! 40

'Tis a pretty Baby-treat;
Nor, I deem, for me unmeet:
Here, for neither Babe or me,
Other Play-mate can I see.
Of the countless living things,
That with stir of feet and wings,
(In the sun or under shade
Upon bough or grassy blade)
And with busy revellings,
Chirp and song, and murmurings, 50
Made this Orchard's narrow space,
And this Vale so blithe a place;
Multitudes are swept away
Never more to breathe the day:
Some are sleeping; some in Bands
Travell'd into distant Lands;
Others slunk to moor and wood,
Far from human neighbourhood,
And, among the Kinds that keep
With us closer fellowship, 60
With us openly abide,
All have laid their mirth aside,
—Where is he that giddy Sprite,
Blue-cap, with his colours bright,
Who was blest as bird could be,
Feeding in the apple-tree,
Made such wanton spoil and rout,
Turning blossoms inside out,

Hung with head towards the ground,
Flutter'd, perch'd; into a round 70
Bound himself, and then unbound;
Lithest, gaudiest Harlequin,
Prettiest Tumbler ever seen,
Light of heart, and light of limb,
What is now become of Him?
Lambs, that through the mountains went
Frisking, bleating merriment,
When the year was in its prime,
They are sober'd by this time.
If you look to vale or hill, 80
If you listen, all is still,
Save a little neighbouring Rill;
That from out the rocky ground
Strikes a solitary sound.
Vainly glitters hill and plain,
And the air is calm in vain;
Vainly Morning spreads the lure
Of a sky serene and pure;
Creature none can she decoy
Into open sign of joy: 90
Is it that they have a fear
Of the dreary season near?
Or that other pleasures be
Sweeter even than gaiety?

Yet, whate'er enjoyments dwell
In the impenetrable cell
Of the silent heart which Nature
Furnishes to every Creature,
Whatsoe'er we feel and know

Too sedate for outward show, 100
Such a light of gladness breaks,
Pretty Kitten! from thy freaks,
Spreads with such a living grace
O'er my little Laura's face;
Yes, the sight so stirs and charms
Thee, Baby, laughing in my arms,
That almost I could repine
That your transports are not mine,
That I do not wholly fare
Even as ye do, thoughtless Pair! 110
And I will have my careless season
Spite of melancholy reason,
Will walk through life in such a way
That, when time brings on decay,
Now and then I may possess
Hours of perfect gladsomeness.
—Pleas'd by any random toy;
By a Kitten's busy joy,
Or an infant's laughing eye
Sharing in the extacy; 120
I would fare like that or this,
Find my wisdom in my bliss;
Keep the sprightly soul awake,
And have faculties to take
Even from things by sorrow wrought
Matter for a jocund thought;
Spite of care, and spite of grief,
To gambol with Life's falling Leaf.

THE SEVEN SISTERS, OR THE SOLITUDE OF BINNORIE.

* * * * *

Seven Daughters had Lord Archibald,
All Children of one Mother:
I could not say in one short day
What love they bore each other,
A Garland of seven Lilies wrought!
Seven Sisters that together dwell;
But he, bold Knight as ever fought,
Their Father, took of them no thought,
He loved the Wars so well.
Sing, mournfully, oh! mournfully, 10
The Solitude of Binnorie!

Fresh blows the wind, a western wind,
And from the shores of Erin,
Across the wave, a Rover brave
To Binnorie is steering:
Right onward to the Scottish strand
The gallant ship is borne;
The Warriors leap upon the land,
And hark! the Leader of the Band
Hath blown his bugle horn. 20
Sing, mournfully, oh! mournfully,
The Solitude of Binnorie.

Beside a Grotto of their own,
With boughs above them closing,
The Seven are laid, and in the shade
They lie like Fawns reposing.
But now, upstarting with affright

At noise of Man and Steed,
Away they fly to left to right—
Of your fair household, Father Knight, 30
Methinks you take small heed!
Sing, mournfully, oh! mournfully,
The Solitude of Binnorie.

Away the seven fair Campbells fly,
And, over Hill and Hollow,
With menace proud, and insult loud,
The youthful Rovers follow.
Cried they, "Your Father loves to roam:
Enough for him to find
The empty House when he comes home; 40
For us your yellow ringlets comb,
For us be fair and kind!"
Sing, mournfully, oh! mournfully,
The Solitude of Binnorie.

Some close behind, some side by side,
Like clouds in stormy weather,
They run, and cry, "Nay let us die,
And let us die together."
A Lake was near; the shore was steep;
There never Foot had been; 50
They ran, and with a desperate leap
Together plung'd into the deep,
Nor ever more were seen.
Sing, mournfully, oh! mournfully,
The Solitude of Binnorie.

The Stream that flows out of the Lake,
As through the glen it rambles,

Repeats a moan o'er moss and stone,
For those seven lovely Campbells.
Seven little Islands, green and bare, 60
Have risen from out the deep:
The Fishers say, those Sisters fair
By Faeries are all buried there,
And there together sleep.
Sing, mournfully, oh! mournfully
The Solitude of Binnorie.

To H. C.,

SIX YEARS OLD.

* * * * *

O Thou! whose fancies from afar are brought;
Who of thy words dost make a mock apparel,
And fittest to unutterable thought
The breeze-like motion and the self-born carol;
Thou Faery Voyager! that dost float
In such clear water, that thy Boat
May rather seem
To brood on air than on an earthly stream;
Suspended in a stream as clear as sky,
Where earth and heaven do make one imagery; 10
O blessed Vision! happy Child!
That art so exquisitely wild,

I think of thee with, many fears
For what may be thy lot in future years.

I thought of times when Pain might be thy guest,
Lord of thy house and hospitality;
And grief, uneasy Lover! never rest
But when she sate within the touch of thee.

Oh! too industrious folly!
Oh! vain and causeless melancholy! 20
Nature will either end thee quite;
Or, lengthening out thy season of delight,
Preserve for thee, by individual right,
A young Lamb's heart among the full-grown flocks.
What hast Thou to do with sorrow,
Or the injuries of tomorrow?

Thou art a Dew-drop, which, the morn brings forth,
Not doom'd to jostle with unkindly shocks;
Or to be trail'd along the soiling earth;
A Gem that glitters while it lives, 30
And no forewarning gives;
But, at the touch of wrong, without a strife
Slips in a moment out of life.

AMONG ALL LOVELY THINGS MY LOVE HAD BEEN

* * * * *

Among all lovely things my Love had been;
Had noted well the stars, all flowers that grew
About her home; but she had never seen
A Glow-worm, never one, and this I knew.

While riding near her home one stormy night
A single Glow-worm did I chance to espy;
I gave a fervent welcome to the sight,
And from my Horse I leapt; great joy had I.

Upon a leaf the Glow-worm did I lay,
To bear it with me through the stormy night: 10
And, as before, it shone without dismay;
Albeit putting forth a fainter light.

When to the Dwelling of my Love I came,
I went into the Orchard quietly;
And left the Glow-worm, blessing it by name,
Laid safely by itself, beneath a Tree.

The whole next day, I hoped, and hoped with fear;
At night the Glow-worm shone beneath the Tree:
I led my Lucy to the spot, "Look here!"
Oh! joy it was for her, and joy for me! 20

I TRAVELL'D AMONG UNKNOWN MEN

* * * * *

I travell'd among unknown Men,
  In Lands beyond the Sea;
Nor England! did I know till then
  What love I bore to thee.

'Tis past, that melancholy dream!
  Nor will I quit thy shore
A second time; for still I seem
  To love thee more and more.

Among thy mountains did I feel
  The joy of my desire; 10
And She I cherish'd turn'd her wheel
  Beside an English fire.

Thy mornings shew'd—thy nights conceal'd
  The bowers where Lucy play'd;
And thine is, too, the last green field
  Which Lucy's eyes survey'd!

ODE TO DUTY.

Stern Daughter of the Voice of God!
O Duty! if that name thou love
Who art a Light to guide, a Rod
To check the erring, and reprove;
Thou who art victory and law
When empty terrors overawe;
From vain temptations dost set free;
From strife and from despair; a glorious ministry.

There are who ask not if thine eye
Be on them; who, in love and truth, 10
Where no misgiving is, rely
Upon the genial sense of youth:
Glad Hearts! without reproach or blot;
Who do thy work, and know it not:
May joy be theirs while life shall last!
And Thou, if they should totter, teach them to stand fast!

Serene will be our days and bright,
And happy will our nature be,
When love is an unerring light,
And joy its own security. 20
And bless'd are they who in the main
This faith, even now, do entertain:
Live in the spirit of this creed;
Yet find that other strength, according to their need.

I, loving freedom, and untried;
No sport of every random gust,

Yet being to myself a guide,
Too blindly have reposed my trust:
Resolved that nothing e'er should press
Upon my present happiness, 30
I shoved unwelcome tasks away;
But thee I now would serve more strictly, if I may.

   Through no disturbance of my soul,
Or strong compunction in me wrought,
I supplicate for thy controul;
But in the quietness of thought:
Me this uncharter'd freedom tires;
I feel the weight of chance desires:
My hopes no more must change their name,
I long for a repose which ever is the same. 40

   Yet not the less would I throughout
Still act according to the voice
Of my own wish; and feel past doubt
That my submissiveness was choice:
Not seeking in the school of pride
For "precepts over dignified,"
Denial and restraint I prize
No farther than they breed a second Will more wise.

   Stern Lawgiver! yet thou dost wear
The Godhead's most benignant grace; 50
Nor know we any thing so fair
As is the smile upon thy face;
Flowers laugh before thee on their beds;
And Fragrance in thy footing treads;
Thou dost preserve the Stars from wrong;

And the most ancient Heavens through Thee are fresh and
strong.

    To humbler functions, awful Power!
I call thee: I myself commend
Unto thy guidance from this hour;
Oh! let my weakness have an end! 60
Give unto me, made lowly wise,
The spirit of self-sacrifice;
The confidence of reason give;
And in the light of truth thy Bondman let me live!

POEMS COMPOSED DURING A TOUR, CHIEFLY ON FOOT.

1. BEGGARS.

She had a tall Man's height, or more;
No bonnet screen'd her from the heat;
A long drab-colour'd Cloak she wore,
A Mantle reaching to her feet:
What other dress she had I could not know;
Only she wore a Cap that was as white as snow.

In all my walks, through field or town,
Such Figure had I never seen:
Her face was of Egyptian brown:
Fit person was she for a Queen, 10
To head those ancient Amazonian files:
Or ruling Bandit's Wife, among the Grecian Isles.

Before me begging did she stand,
Pouring out sorrows like a sea;
Grief after grief:—on English Land
Such woes I knew could never be;
And yet a boon I gave her; for the Creature
Was beautiful to see; a Weed of glorious feature!

I left her, and pursued my way;
And soon before me did espy 20
A pair of little Boys at play,

Chasing a crimson butterfly;
The Taller follow'd with his hat in hand,
Wreath'd round with yellow flow'rs, the gayest of the land.

The Other wore a rimless crown,
With leaves of laurel stuck about:
And they both follow'd up and down,
Each whooping with a merry shout;
Two Brothers seem'd they, eight and ten years old;
And like that Woman's face as gold is like to gold. 30

They bolted on me thus, and lo!
Each ready with a plaintive whine;
Said I, "Not half an hour ago
Your Mother has had alms of mine."
"That cannot be," one answer'd, "She is dead."
"Nay but I gave her pence, and she will buy you bread."

"She has been dead, Sir, many a day."
"Sweet Boys, you're telling me a lie";
"It was your Mother, as I say—"
And in the twinkling of an eye, 40
"Come, come!" cried one; and, without more ado,
Off to some other play they both together flew.

2. TO A SKY-LARK.

Up with me! up with me into the clouds!
For thy song, Lark, is strong;
Up with me, up with me into the clouds!

Singing, singing,
With all the heav'ns about thee ringing,
  Lift me, guide me, till I find
That spot which seems so to thy mind!

  I have walk'd through wildernesses dreary,
  And today my heart is weary;
  Had I now the soul of a Faery, 10
    Up to thee would I fly.
There is madness about thee, and joy divine
    In that song of thine;
Up with me, up with me, high and high,
To thy banqueting-place in the sky! 15
    Joyous as Morning,
  Thou art laughing and scorning;
Thou hast a nest, for thy love and thy rest:
And, though little troubled with sloth,
Drunken Lark! thou would'st be loth 20
To be such a Traveller as I.
  Happy, happy Liver!
With a soul as strong as a mountain River,
Pouring out praise to the Almighty Giver,
  Joy and jollity be with us both!
  Hearing thee, or else some other,
    As merry a Brother,
I on the earth will go plodding on,
By myself, chearfully, till the day is done.

3. WITH HOW SAD STEPS, O MOON, THOU CLIMB'ST THE SKY

3.

"With how sad steps, O Moon thou climb'st the sky.
How silently, and with how wan a face!" [2]
Where art thou? Thou whom I have seen on high
Running among the clouds a Wood-nymph's race?
Unhappy Nuns, whose common breath's a sigh
Which they would stifle, move at such a pace!
The Northern Wind, to call thee to the chace,
Must blow tonight his bugle horn. Had I
The power of Merlin, Goddess! this should be
And all the Stars, now shrouded up in heaven,
Should sally forth to keep thee company.
What strife would then be yours, fair Creatures, driv'n
Now up, now down, and sparkling in your glee!
But, Cynthia, should to Thee the palm be giv'n,
Queen both for beauty and for majesty.

[Footnote 2: From a sonnet of Sir Philip Sydney.]

4. ALICE FELL.

The Post-boy drove with fierce career,
For threat'ning clouds the moon had drown'd;
When suddenly I seem'd to hear
A moan, a lamentable sound.

As if the wind blew many ways
I heard the sound, and more and more:
It seem'd to follow with the Chaise,
And still I heard it as before.

At length I to the Boy call'd out,
He stopp'd his horses at the word; 10
But neither cry, nor voice, nor shout,
Nor aught else like it could be heard.

The Boy then smack'd his whip, and fast
The horses scamper'd through the rain;
And soon I heard upon the blast
The voice, and bade him halt again.

Said I, alighting on the ground,
"What can it be, this piteous moan?"
And there a little Girl I found,
Sitting behind the Chaise, alone. 20

"My Cloak!" the word was last and first,
And loud and bitterly she wept,
As if her very heart would burst;
And down from off the Chaise she leapt.

"What ails you, Child?" she sobb'd, "Look here!"
I saw it in the wheel entangled,
A weather beaten Rag as e'er
From any garden scare-crow dangled.

'Twas twisted betwixt nave and spoke;
Her help she lent, and with good heed 30

Together we released the Cloak;
A wretched, wretched rag indeed!

"And whither are you going, Child,
To night along these lonesome ways?"
"To Durham" answer'd she half wild—
"Then come with me into the chaise."

She sate like one past all relief;
Sob after sob she forth did send
In wretchedness, as if her grief
Could never, never, have an end. 40

"My Child, in Durham do you dwell?"
She check'd herself in her distress,
And said, "My name is Alice Fell;
I'm fatherless and motherless."

"And I to Durham, Sir, belong."
And then, as if the thought would choke
Her very heart, her grief grew strong;
And all was for her tatter'd Cloak.

The chaise drove on; our journey's end
Was nigh; and, sitting by my side, 50
As if she'd lost her only friend
She wept, nor would be pacified.

Up to the Tavern-door we post;
Of Alice and her grief I told;
And I gave money to the Host,
To buy a new Cloak for the old.

"And let it be of duffil grey,
As warm a cloak as man can sell!"
Proud Creature was she the next day,
The little Orphan, Alice Fell! 60

5. RESOLUTION AND INDEPENDENCE.

There was a roaring in the wind all night;
The rain came heavily and fell in floods;
But now the sun is rising calm and bright;
The birds are singing in the distant woods;
Over his own sweet voice the Stock-dove broods;
The Jay makes answer as the Magpie chatters;
And all the air is fill'd with pleasant noise of waters.

All things that love the sun are out of doors;
The sky rejoices in the morning's birth;
The grass is bright with rain-drops; on the moors 10
The Hare is running races in her mirth;
And with her feet she from the plashy earth
Raises a mist; which, glittering in the sun,
Runs with her all the way, wherever she doth run.

I was a Traveller then upon the moor;
I saw the Hare that rac'd about with joy;
I heard the woods, and distant waters, roar;
Or heard them not, as happy as a Boy:
The pleasant season did my heart employ:
My old remembrances went from me wholly; 20
And all the ways of men, so vain and melancholy.

But, as it sometimes chanceth, from the might
Of joy in minds that can no farther go,
As high as we have mounted in delight
In our dejection do we sink as low,
To me that morning did it happen so;
And fears, and fancies, thick upon me came;
Dim sadness, & blind thoughts I knew not nor could name.

I heard the Sky-lark singing in the sky;
And I bethought me of the playful Hare: 30
Even such a happy Child of earth am I;
Even as these blissful Creatures do I fare;
Far from the world I walk, and from all care;
But there may come another day to me,
Solitude, pain of heart, distress, and poverty.

My whole life I have liv'd in pleasant thought,
As if life's business were a summer mood;
As if all needful things would come unsought
To genial faith, still rich in genial good;
But how can He expect that others should 40
Build for him, sow for him, and at his call
Love him, who for himself will take no heed at all?

I thought of Chatterton, the marvellous Boy,
The sleepless Soul that perish'd in its pride;
Of Him who walk'd in glory and in joy
Behind his plough, upon the mountain-side:
By our own spirits are we deified;
We Poets in our youth begin in gladness;
But thereof comes in the end despondency and madness.

Now, whether it were by peculiar grace, 50
A leading from above, a something given,
Yet it befel, that, in this lonely place,
When up and down my fancy thus was driven,
And I with these untoward thoughts had striven,
I saw a Man before me unawares:
The oldest Man he seem'd that ever wore grey hairs.

My course I stopped as soon as I espied
The Old Man in that naked wilderness:
Close by a Pond, upon the further side,
He stood alone: a minute's space I guess 60
I watch'd him, he continuing motionless:
To the Pool's further margin then I drew;
He being all the while before me full in view.

As a huge Stone is sometimes seen to lie
Couch'd on the bald top of an eminence;
Wonder to all who do the same espy
By what means it could thither come, and whence;
So that it seems a thing endued with sense:
Like a Sea-beast crawl'd forth, which on a shelf
Of rock or sand reposeth, there to sun itself. 70

Such seem'd this Man, not all alive nor dead,
Nor all asleep; in his extreme old age:
His body was bent double, feet and head
Coming together in their pilgrimage;
As if some dire constraint of pain, or rage
Of sickness felt by him in times long past,
A more than human weight upon his frame had cast.

Himself he propp'd, his body, limbs, and face,
Upon a long grey Staff of shaven wood:
And, still as I drew near with gentle pace, 80
Beside the little pond or moorish flood
Motionless as a Cloud the Old Man stood;
That heareth not the loud winds when they call;
And moveth altogether, if it move at all.

At length, himself unsettling, he the Pond
Stirred with his Staff, and fixedly did look
Upon the muddy water, which he conn'd,
As if he had been reading in a book:
And now such freedom as I could I took;
And, drawing to his side, to him did say, 90
"This morning gives us promise of a glorious day."

A gentle answer did the Old Man make,
In courteous speech which forth he slowly drew:
And him with further words I thus bespake,
"What kind of work is that which you pursue?
This is a lonesome place for one like you."
He answer'd me with pleasure and surprize;
And there was, while he spake, a fire about his eyes.

His words came feebly, from a feeble chest,
Yet each in solemn order follow'd each, 100
With something of a lofty utterance drest;
Choice word, and measured phrase; above the reach
Of ordinary men; a stately speech!
Such as grave Livers do in Scotland use,
Religious men, who give to God and Man their dues.

He told me that he to this pond had come
To gather Leeches, being old and poor:
Employment hazardous and wearisome!
And he had many hardships to endure:
From Pond to Pond he roam'd, from moor to moor, 110
Housing, with God's good help, by choice or chance:
And in this way he gain'd an honest maintenance.

The Old Man still stood talking by my side;
But now his voice to me was like a stream
Scarce heard; nor word from word could I divide;
And the whole Body of the man did seem
Like one whom I had met with in a dream;
Or like a Man from some far region sent;
To give me human strength, and strong admonishment.

My former thoughts return'd: the fear that kills; 120
The hope that is unwilling to be fed;
Cold, pain, and labour, and all fleshly ills;
And mighty Poets in their misery dead.
And now, not knowing what the Old Man had said,
My question eagerly did I renew,
"How is it that you live, and what is it you do?"

He with a smile did then his words repeat;
And said, that, gathering Leeches, far and wide
He travelled; stirring thus about his feet
The waters of the Ponds where they abide. 130
"Once I could meet with them on every side;
But they have dwindled long by slow decay;
Yet still I persevere, and find them where I may."

While he was talking thus, the lonely place,
The Old Man's shape, and speech, all troubled me:
In my mind's eye I seem'd to see him pace
About the weary moors continually,
Wandering about alone and silently.
While I these thoughts within myself pursued,
He, having made a pause, the same discourse renewed. 140

And soon with this he other matter blended,
Chearfully uttered, with demeanour kind,
But stately in the main; and, when he ended,
I could have laugh'd myself to scorn, to find
In that decrepit Man so firm a mind.
"God," said I, "be my help and stay secure;
I'll think of the Leech-gatherer on the lonely moor."

SONNETS.

PREFATORY SONNET.

* * * * *

Nuns fret not at their Convent's narrow room;
And Hermits are contented with their Cells;
And Students with their pensive Citadels:
Maids at the Wheel, the Weaver at his Loom,
Sit blithe and happy; Bees that soar for bloom,
High as the highest Peak of Furness Fells,
Will murmur by the hour in Foxglove bells:
In truth, the prison, unto which we doom
Ourselves, no prison is: and hence to me,
In sundry moods, 'twas pastime to be bound
Within the Sonnet's scanty plot of ground:
Pleas'd if some Souls (for such there needs must be)
Who have felt the weight of too much liberty,
Should find short solace there, as I have found.

PART THE FIRST.

* * * * *

MISCELLANEOUS SONNETS.

1.

* * * * *

How sweet it is, when mother Fancy rocks
The wayward brain, to saunter through a wood!
An old place, full of many a lovely brood,
Tall trees, green arbours, and ground flowers in flocks;
And Wild rose tip-toe upon hawthorn stocks,
Like to a bonny Lass, who plays her pranks
At Wakes and Fairs with wandering Mountebanks,
When she stands cresting the Clown's head, and mocks
The crowd beneath her. Verily I think,
Such place to me is sometimes like a dream
Or map of the whole world: thoughts, link by link
Enter through ears and eyesight, with such gleam
Of all things, that at last in fear I shrink,
And leap at once from the delicious stream.

2.

Where lies the Land to which yon Ship must go?
Festively she puts forth in trim array;
As vigorous as a Lark at break of day:
Is she for tropic suns, or polar snow?
What boots the enquiry? Neither friend nor foe
She cares for; let her travel where she may,
She finds familiar names, a beaten way
Ever before her, and a wind to blow.
Yet still I ask, what Haven is her mark?
And, almost as it was when ships were rare,
From time to time, like Pilgrims, here and there
Crossing the waters; doubt, and something dark,
Of the old Sea some reverential fear,
Is with me at thy farewell, joyous Bark!

3. COMPOSED AFTER A JOURNEY ACROSS THE HAMILTON HILLS, YORKSHIRE.

Ere we had reach'd the wish'd-for place, night fell:
We were too late at least by one dark hour,
And nothing could we see of all that power
Of prospect, whereof many thousands tell.
The western sky did recompence us well
With Grecian Temple, Minaret, and Bower;

And, in one part, a Minster with its Tower
Substantially distinct, a place for Bell
Or Clock to toll from. Many a glorious pile
Did we behold, sights that might well repay
All disappointment! and, as such, the eye
Delighted in them; but we felt, the while,
We should forget them: they are of the sky,
And from our earthly memory fade away.

4.

....they are of the sky,
And from our earthly memory fade away.

  These words were utter'd in a pensive mood,
Even while mine eyes were on that solemn sight:
A contrast and reproach to gross delight,
And life's unspiritual pleasures daily woo'd!
But now upon this thought I cannot brood:
It is unstable, and deserts me quite;
Nor will I praise a Cloud, however bright,
Disparaging Man's gifts, and proper food.
The Grove, the sky-built Temple, and the Dome,
Though clad in colours beautiful and pure,
Find in the heart of man no natural home:
The immortal Mind craves objects that endure:
These cleave to it; from these it cannot roam,
Nor they from it: their fellowship is secure.

5. TO SLEEP.

O gentle Sleep! do they belong to thee,
These twinklings of oblivion? Thou dost love
To sit in meekness, like the brooding Dove,
A Captive never wishing to be free.
This tiresome night, O Sleep! thou art to me
A Fly, that up and down himself doth shove
Upon a fretful rivulet, now above,
Now on the water vex'd with mockery.
I have no pain that calls for patience, no;
Hence am I cross and peevish as a child:
Am pleas'd by fits to have thee for my foe,
Yet ever willing to be reconciled:
O gentle Creature! do not use me so,
But once and deeply let me be beguiled.

6. TO SLEEP.

A flock of sheep that leisurely pass by,
One after one; the sound of rain, and bees
Murmuring; the fall of rivers, winds and seas,
Smooth fields, white sheets of water, and pure sky;
I've thought of all by turns; and still I lie
Sleepless; and soon the small birds' melodies
Must hear, first utter'd from my orchard trees;
And the first Cuckoo's melancholy cry.
Even thus last night, and two nights more, I lay,
And could not win thee, Sleep! by any stealth:
So do not let me wear to night away:

Without Thee what is all the morning's wealth?
Come, blessed barrier betwixt day and day,
Dear mother of fresh thoughts and joyous health!

7. TO SLEEP.

Fond words have oft been spoken to thee, Sleep!
And thou hast had thy store of tenderest names;
The very sweetest words that fancy frames
When thankfulness of heart is strong and deep!
Dear bosom Child we call thee, that dost steep
In rich reward all suffering; Balm that tames
All anguish; Saint that evil thoughts and aims
Takest away, and into souls dost creep,
Like to a breeze from heaven. Shall I alone;
I surely not a man ungently made,
Call thee worst Tyrant by which Flesh is crost?
Perverse, self-will'd to own and to disown,
Mere Slave of them who never for thee pray'd,
Still last to come where thou art wanted most!

8.

With Ships the sea was sprinkled far and nigh,
Like stars in heaven, and joyously it showed;
Some lying fast at anchor in the road,
Some veering up and down, one knew not why.

A goodly Vessel did I then espy
Come like a Giant from a haven broad;
And lustily along the Bay she strode,
Her tackling rich, and of apparel high.
This Ship was nought to me, nor I to her,
Yet I pursued her with a Lover's look;
This Ship to all the rest did I prefer:
When will she turn, and whither? She will brook
No tarrying; where she comes the winds must stir:
On went She, and due north her journey took.

9. TO THE RIVER DUDDON.

O mountain Stream! the Shepherd and his Cot
Are privileg'd Inmates of deep solitude:
Nor would the nicest Anchorite exclude
A Field or two of brighter green, or Plot
Of tillage-ground, that seemeth like a spot
Of stationary sunshine: thou hast view'd
These only, Duddon! with their paths renew'd
By fits and starts, yet this contents thee not.
Thee hath some awful Spirit impell'd to leave,
Utterly to desert, the haunts of men,
Though simple thy Companions were and few;
And through this wilderness a passage cleave
Attended but by thy own Voice, save when
The Clouds and Fowls of the air thy way pursue.

10. FROM THE ITALIAN OF MICHAEL ANGELO.

Yes! hope may with my strong desire keep pace,
And I be undeluded, unbetray'd;
For if of our affections none find grace
In sight of Heaven, then, wherefore hath God made
The world which we inhabit? Better plea
Love cannot have, than that in loving thee
Glory to that eternal Peace is paid,
Who such Divinity to thee imparts
As hallows and makes pure all gentle hearts.
His hope is treacherous only whose love dies
With beauty, which is varying every hour;
But, in chaste hearts uninfluenced by the power
Of outward change, there blooms a deathless flower,
That breathes on earth the air of paradise.

11. FROM THE SAME.

No mortal object did these eyes behold
When first they met the placid light of thine,
And my Soul felt her destiny divine,
And hope of endless peace in me grew bold:
Heav'n-born, the Soul a heav'n-ward course must hold;
Beyond the visible world She soars to seek,
For what delights the sense is false and weak,
Ideal Form, the universal mould.
The wise man, I affirm, can find no rest
In that which perishes: nor will he lend
His heart to aught which doth on time depend.

'Tis sense, unbridled will, and not true love,
Which kills the soul: Love betters what is best,
Even here below, but more in heaven above.

12. FROM THE SAME.

TO THE SUPREME BEING.

The prayers I make will then be sweet indeed
If Thou the spirit give by which I pray:
My unassisted heart is barren clay,
Which of its native self can nothing feed:
Of good and pious works thou art the seed,
Which quickens only where thou say'st it may:
Unless thou shew to us thine own true way
No man can find it: Father! thou must lead.
Do Thou, then, breathe those thoughts into my mind
By which such virtue may in me be bred
That in thy holy footsteps I may tread;
The fetters of my tongue do Thou unbind,
That I may have the power to sing of thee,
And sound thy praises everlastingly.

13.

WRITTEN IN VERY EARLY YOUTH.

Calm is all nature as a resting wheel.
The Kine are couch'd upon the dewy grass;
The Horse alone, seen dimly as I pass,
Is up, and cropping yet his later meal:
Dark is the ground; a slumber seems to steal
O'er vale, and mountain, and the starless sky.
Now, in this blank of things, a harmony
Home-felt, and home-created seems to heal
That grief for which the senses still supply
Fresh food; for only then, when memory
Is hush'd, am I at rest. My Friends, restrain
Those busy cares that would allay my pain:
Oh! leave me to myself; nor let me feel
The officious touch that makes me droop again.

14. COMPOSED UPON WESTMINSTER BRIDGE,
SEPT. 3, 1803.

Earth has not any thing to shew more fair:
Dull would he be of soul who could pass by
A sight so touching in its majesty:
This City now doth like a garment wear
The beauty of the morning; silent, bare,
Ships, towers, domes, theatres, and temples lie
Open unto the fields, and to the sky;
All bright and glittering in the smokeless air.

Never did sun more beautifully steep
In his first splendor valley, rock, or hill;
Ne'er saw I, never felt, a calm so deep!
The river glideth at his own sweet will:
Dear God! the very houses seem asleep;
And all that mighty heart is lying still!

15.

"Beloved Vale!" I said, "when I shall con
Those many records of my childish years,
Remembrance of myself and of my peers
Will press me down: to think of what is gone
Will be an awful thought, if life have one."
But, when into the Vale I came, no fears
Distress'd me; I look'd round, I shed no tears;
Deep thought, or awful vision, I had none.
By thousand petty fancies I was cross'd,
To see the Trees, which I had thought so tall,
Mere dwarfs; the Brooks so narrow, Fields so small.
A Juggler's Balls old Time about him toss'd;
I looked, I stared, I smiled, I laughed; and all
The weight of sadness was in wonder lost.

16.

Methought I saw the footsteps of a throne
Which mists and vapours from mine eyes did shroud,
Nor view of him who sate thereon allow'd;
But all the steps and ground about were strown
With sights the ruefullest that flesh and bone
Ever put on; a miserable crowd,
Sick, hale, old, young, who cried before that cloud,
"Thou art our king, O Death! to thee we groan."
I seem'd to mount those steps; the vapours gave
Smooth way; and I beheld the face of one
Sleeping alone within a mossy cave,
With her face up to heaven; that seem'd to have
Pleasing remembrance of a thought foregone;
A lovely Beauty in a summer grave!

17. TO THE ——.

Lady! the songs of Spring were in the grove
While I was framing beds for winter flowers;
While I was planting green unfading bowers,
And shrubs to hang upon the warm alcove,
And sheltering wall; and still, as fancy wove
The dream, to time and nature's blended powers
I gave this paradise for winter hours,
A labyrinth Lady! which your feet shall rove.
Yes! when the sun of life more feebly shines,
Becoming thoughts, I trust, of solemn gloom

Or of high gladness you shall hither bring;
And these perennial bowers and murmuring pines
Be gracious as the music and the bloom
And all the mighty ravishment of Spring.

18.

The world is too much with us; late and soon,
Getting and spending, we lay waste our powers:
Little we see in nature that is ours;
We have given our hearts away, a sordid boon!
This Sea that bares her bosom to the moon;
The Winds that will be howling at all hours
And are up-gathered now like sleeping flowers;
For this, for every thing, we are out of tune;
It moves us not—Great God! I'd rather be
A Pagan suckled in a creed outworn;
So might I, standing on this pleasant lea,
Have glimpses that would make me less forlorn;
Have sight of Proteus coming from the sea;
Or hear old Triton blow his wreathed horn.

19.

It is a beauteous Evening, calm and free;
The holy time is quiet as a Nun
Breathless with adoration; the broad sun
Is sinking down in its tranquillity;
The gentleness of heaven is on the Sea:
Listen! the mighty Being is awake
And doth with his eternal motion make
A sound like thunder—everlastingly.
Dear Child! dear Girl! that walkest with me here,
If thou appear'st untouch'd by solemn thought,
Thy nature is not therefore less divine:
Thou liest in Abraham's bosom all the year;
And worshipp'st at the Temple's inner shrine,
God being with thee when we know it not.

20. TO THE MEMORY OF *RAISLEY CALVERT*.

Calvert! it must not be unheard by them
Who may respect my name that I to thee
Ow'd many years of early liberty.
This care was thine when sickness did condemn
Thy youth to hopeless wasting, root and stem:
That I, if frugal and severe, might stray
Where'er I liked; and finally array
My temples with the Muse's diadem.
Hence, if in freedom I have lov'd the truth,
If there be aught of pure, or good, or great,
In my past verse; or shall be, in the lays

Of higher mood, which now I meditate,
It gladdens me, O worthy, short-lived Youth!
To think how much of this will be thy praise.

END OF THE FIRST PART.

PART THE SECOND.

SONNETS

DEDICATED TO LIBERTY.

1. COMPOSED BY THE *SEA-SIDE, NEAR CALAIS,* AUGUST, 1802.

Fair Star of Evening, Splendor of the West,
Star of my Country! on the horizon's brink
Thou hangest, stooping, as might seem, to sink
On England's bosom; yet well pleas'd to rest,
Meanwhile, and be to her a glorious crest
Conspicuous to the Nations. Thou, I think,
Should'st be my Country's emblem; and should'st wink,
Bright Star! with laughter on her banners, drest
In thy fresh beauty. There! that dusky spot
Beneath thee, it is England; there it lies.
Blessings be on you both! one hope, one lot,
One life, one glory! I, with many a fear
For my dear Country, many heartfelt sighs,
Among Men who do not love her linger here.

2. CALAIS, AUGUST, 1802.

Is it a Reed that's shaken by the wind,
Or what is it that ye go forth to see?
Lords, Lawyers, Statesmen, Squires of low degree,
Men known, and men unknown, Sick, Lame, and Blind,
Post forward all, like Creatures of one kind,
With first-fruit offerings crowd to bend the knee
In France, before the new-born Majesty.
'Tis ever thus. Ye Men of prostrate mind!
A seemly reverence may be paid to power;
But that's a loyal virtue, never sown
In haste, nor springing with a transient shower:
When truth, when sense, when liberty were flown
What hardship had it been to wait an hour?
Shame on you, feeble Heads, to slavery prone!

3. TO A FRIEND, COMPOSED NEAR CALAIS, ON THE ROAD LEADING TO ARDRES, AUGUST 7TH, 1802.

Jones! when from Calais southward you and I
Travell'd on foot together; then this Way,
Which I am pacing now, was like the May
With festivals of new-born Liberty:
A homeless sound of joy was in the Sky;
The antiquated Earth, as one might say,
Beat like the heart of Man: songs, garlands, play,
Banners, and happy faces, far and nigh!
And now, sole register that these things were,
Two solitary greetings have I heard,

"*Good morrow, Citizen*!" a hollow word,
As if a dead Man spake it! Yet despair
I feel not: happy am I as a Bird:
Fair seasons yet will come, and hopes as fair.

4.

  I griev'd for Buonaparte, with a vain
And an unthinking grief! the vital blood
Of that Man's mind what can it be? What food
Fed his first hopes? What knowledge could He gain?
'Tis not in battles that from youth we train
The Governor who must be wise and good,
And temper with the sternness of the brain
Thoughts motherly, and meek as womanhood.
Wisdom doth live with children round her knees:
Books, leisure, perfect freedom, and the talk
Man holds with week-day man in the hourly walk
Of the mind's business: these are the degrees
By which true Sway doth mount; this is the stalk
True Power doth grow on; and her rights are these.

5. *CALAIS.* AUGUST 15TH, 1802.

Festivals have I seen that were not names:
This is young Buonaparte's natal day;
And his is henceforth an established sway,
Consul for life. With worship France proclaims
Her approbation, and with pomps and games.
Heaven grant that other Cities may be gay!
Calais is not: and I have bent my way
To the Sea-coast, noting that each man frames
His business as he likes. Another time
That was, when I was here long years ago:
The senselessness of joy was then sublime!
Happy is he, who, caring not for Pope,
Consul, or King, can sound himself to know
The destiny of Man, and live in hope.

6. ON THE EXTINCTION OF THE *VENETIAN REPUBLIC.*

Once did She hold the gorgeous East in fee;
And was the safeguard of the West: the worth
Of Venice did not fall below her birth,
Venice, the eldest Child of Liberty.
She was a Maiden City, bright and free;
No guile seduced, no force could violate;
And when She took unto herself a Mate
She must espouse the everlasting Sea.
And what if she had seen those glories fade,
Those titles vanish, and that strength decay,

Yet shall some tribute of regret be paid
When her long life hath reach'd its final day:
Men are we, and must grieve when even the Shade
Of that which once was great is pass'd away.

7. THE KING OF SWEDEN.

The Voice of Song from distant lands shall call
To that great King; shall hail the crowned Youth
Who, taking counsel of unbending Truth,
By one example hath set forth to all
How they with dignity may stand; or fall,
If fall they must. Now, whither doth it tend?
And what to him and his shall be the end?
That thought is one which neither can appal
Nor chear him; for the illustrious Swede hath done
The thing which ought to be: He stands *above*
All consequences: work he hath begun
Of fortitude, and piety, and love,
Which all his glorious Ancestors approve:
The Heroes bless him, him their rightful Son.

8. TO TOUSSAINT L'OUVERTURE.

Toussaint, the most unhappy Man of Men!
Whether the rural Milk-maid by her Cow
Sing in thy hearing, or thou liest now

Alone in some deep dungeon's earless den,
O miserable chieftain! where and when
Wilt thou find patience? Yet die not; do thou
Wear rather in thy bonds a chearful brow:
Though fallen Thyself, never to rise again,
Live, and take comfort. Thou hast left behind
Powers that will work for thee; air, earth, and skies;
There's not a breathing of the common wind
That will forget thee; thou hast great allies;
Thy friends are exultations, agonies,
And love, and Man's unconquerable mind.

9.

September 1st, 1802.

We had a fellow-Passenger who came
From Calais with us, gaudy in array,
A Negro Woman like a Lady gay,
Yet silent as a woman fearing blame;
Dejected, meek, yea pitiably tame,
She sate, from notice turning not away,
But on our proffer'd kindness still did lay
A weight of languid speech, or at the same
Was silent, motionless in eyes and face.
She was a Negro Woman driv'n from France,
Rejected like all others of that race,
Not one of whom may now find footing there;

This the poor Out-cast did to us declare,
Nor murmur'd at the unfeeling Ordinance.

10. COMPOSED IN THE *VALLEY, NEAR DOVER*, ON THE DAY OF LANDING.

Dear fellow Traveller! here we are once more.
The Cock that crows, the Smoke that curls, that sound
Of Bells, those Boys that in yon meadow-ground
In white sleev'd shirts are playing by the score,
And even this little River's gentle roar,
All, all are English. Oft have I look'd round
With joy in Kent's green vales; but never found
Myself so satisfied in heart before.
Europe is yet in Bonds; but let that pass,
Thought for another moment. Thou art free
My Country! and 'tis joy enough and pride
For one hour's perfect bliss, to tread the grass
Of England once again, and hear and see,
With such a dear Companion at my side.

11.

September, 1802.

Inland, within a hollow Vale, I stood,
And saw, while sea was calm and air was clear,
The Coast of France, the Coast of France how near!
Drawn almost into frightful neighbourhood.
I shrunk, for verily the barrier flood
Was like a Lake, or River bright and fair,
A span of waters; yet what power is there!
What mightiness for evil and for good!
Even so doth God protect us if we be
Virtuous and wise: Winds blow, and Waters roll,
Strength to the brave, and Power, and Deity,
Yet in themselves are nothing! One decree
Spake laws to *them*, and said that by the Soul
Only the Nations shall be great and free.

12. THOUGHT OF A BRITON ON THE *SUBJUGATION OF SWITZERLAND*.

Two Voices are there; one is of the Sea,
One of the Mountains; each a mighty Voice:
In both from age to age Thou didst rejoice,
They were thy chosen Music, Liberty!
There came a Tyrant, and with holy glee
Thou fought'st against Him; but hast vainly striven;
Thou from thy Alpine Holds at length art driven,
Where not a torrent murmurs heard by thee.

Of one deep bliss thine ear hath been bereft:
Then cleave, O cleave to that which still is left!
For, high-soul'd Maid, what sorrow would it be
That mountain Floods should thunder as before,
And Ocean bellow from his rocky shore,
And neither awful Voice be heard by thee!

13. WRITTEN IN LONDON, SEPTEMBER, 1802.

O Friend! I know not which way I must look
For comfort, being, as I am, opprest,
To think that now our Life is only drest
For shew; mean handywork of craftsman, cook,
Or groom! We must run glittering like a Brook
In the open sunshine, or we are unblest:
The wealthiest man among us is the best:
No grandeur now in nature or in book
Delights us. Rapine, avarice, expence,
This is idolatry; and these we adore:
Plain living and high thinking are no more:
The homely beauty of the good old cause
Is gone; our peace, our fearful innocence,
And pure religion breathing household laws.

14.

LONDON, 1802.

Milton! thou should'st be living at this hour:
England hath need of thee: she is a fen
Of stagnant waters: altar, sword and pen,
Fireside, the heroic wealth of hall and bower,
Have forfeited their ancient English dower
Of inward happiness. We are selfish men;
Oh! raise us up, return to us again;
And give us manners, virtue, freedom, power.
Thy soul was like a Star and dwelt apart:
Thou hadst a voice whose sound was like the sea;
Pure as the naked heavens, majestic, free,
So didst thou travel on life's common way,
In chearful godliness; and yet thy heart
The lowliest duties on itself did lay.

15.

Great Men have been among us; hands that penn'd
And tongues that utter'd wisdom, better none:
The later Sydney, Marvel, Harrington,
Young Vane, and others who call'd Milton Friend.
These Moralists could act and comprehend:
They knew how genuine glory was put on;
Taught us how rightfully a nation shone
In splendor: what strength was, that would not bend
But in magnanimous meekness. France, 'tis strange,

Hath brought forth no such souls as we had then.
Perpetual emptiness! unceasing change!
No single Volume paramount, no code,
No master spirit, no determined road;
But equally a want of Books and Men!

16.

It is not to be thought of that the Flood
Of British freedom, which to the open Sea
Of the world's praise from dark antiquity
Hath flowed, "with pomp of waters, unwithstood,"
Road by which all might come and go that would,
And bear out freights of worth to foreign lands;
That this most famous Stream in Bogs and Sands
Should perish; and to evil and to good
Be lost for ever. In our Halls is hung
Armoury of the invincible Knights of old:
We must be free or die, who speak the tongue
That Shakespeare spake; the faith and morals hold
Which Milton held. In every thing we are sprung
Of Earth's first blood, have titles manifold.

17.

When I have borne in memory what has tamed
Great Nations, how ennobling thoughts depart
When Men change Swords for Ledgers, and desert
The Student's bower for gold, some fears unnamed
I had, my Country! am I to be blamed?
But, when I think of Thee, and what Thou art,
Verily, in the bottom of my heart,
Of those unfilial fears I am ashamed.
But dearly must we prize thee; we who find
In thee a bulwark of the cause of men;
And I by my affection was beguiled.
What wonder, if a Poet, now and then,
Among the many movements of his mind,
Felt for thee as a Lover or a Child.

18.

October, 1803.

One might believe that natural miseries
Had blasted France, and made of it a land
Unfit for Men; and that in one great Band
Her Sons were bursting forth, to dwell at ease.
But 'tis a chosen soil, where sun and breeze
Shed gentle favors; rural works are there;
And ordinary business without care;
Spot rich in all things that can soothe and please!
How piteous then that there should be such dearth

Of knowledge; that whole myriads should unite
To work against themselves such fell despite:
Should come in phrenzy and in drunken mirth,
Impatient to put out the only light
Of Liberty that yet remains on Earth!

19.

There is a bondage which is worse to bear
Than his who breathes, by roof, and floor, and wall,
Pent in, a Tyrant's solitary Thrall:
'Tis his who walks about in the open air,
One of a Nation who, henceforth, must wear
Their fetters in their Souls. For who could be,
Who, even the best, in such condition, free
From self-reproach, reproach which he must share
With Human Nature? Never be it ours
To see the Sun how brightly it will shine,
And know that noble Feelings, manly Powers,
Instead of gathering strength must droop and pine,
And Earth with all her pleasant fruits and flowers
Fade, and participate in Man's decline.

20.

October, 1803.

These times touch money'd Worldlings with dismay:
Even rich men, brave by nature, taint the air
With words of apprehension and despair:
While tens of thousands, thinking on the affray,
Men unto whom sufficient for the day
And minds not stinted or untill'd are given,
Sound, healthy Children of the God of Heaven,
Are cheerful as the rising Sun in May.
What do we gather hence but firmer faith
That every gift of noble origin
Is breathed upon by Hope's perpetual breath;
That virtue and the faculties within
Are vital, and that riches are akin
To fear, to change, to cowardice, and death!

21.

England! the time is come when thou shouldst wean
Thy heart from its emasculating food;
The truth should now be better understood;
Old things have been unsettled; we have seen
Fair seed-time, better harvest might have been
But for thy trespasses; and, at this day,
If for Greece, Egypt, India, Africa,
Aught good were destined, Thou wouldst step between.
England! all nations in this charge agree:

But worse, more ignorant in love and hate,
Far, far more abject is thine Enemy:
Therefore the wise pray for thee, though the freight
Of thy offences be a heavy weight:
Oh grief! that Earth's best hopes rest all with Thee!

22.

October, 1803.

When, looking on the present face of things,
I see one Man, of Men the meanest too!
Rais'd up to sway the World, to do, undo,
With mighty Nations for his Underlings,
The great events with which old story rings
Seem vain and hollow; I find nothing great;
Nothing is left which I can venerate;
So that almost a doubt within me springs
Of Providence, such emptiness at length
Seems at the heart of all things. But, great God!
I measure back the steps which I have trod,
And tremble, seeing, as I do, the strength
Of such poor Instruments, with thoughts sublime
I tremble at the sorrow of the time.

23. TO THE MEN OF KENT.

October, 1803.

Vanguard of Liberty, ye Men of Kent,
Ye Children of a Soil that doth advance
It's haughty brow against the coast of France,
Now is the time to prove your hardiment!
To France be words of invitation sent!
They from their Fields can see the countenance
Of your fierce war, may ken the glittering lance.
And hear you shouting forth your brave intent.
Left single, in bold parley, Ye, of yore,
Did from the Norman win a gallant wreath;
Confirm'd the charters that were yours before;—
No parleying now! In Britain is one breath;
We all are with you now from Shore to Shore:—
Ye Men of Kent, 'tis Victory or Death!

24.

October, 1803.

Six thousand Veterans practis'd in War's game,
Tried Men, at Killicranky were array'd
Against an equal Host that wore the Plaid,
Shepherds and Herdsmen.—Like a whirlwind came
The Highlanders, the slaughter spread like flame;
And Garry thundering down his mountain-road
Was stopp'd, and could not breathe beneath the load

Of the dead bodies. 'Twas a day of shame
For them whom precept and the pedantry
Of cold mechanic battle do enslave.
Oh! for a single hour of that Dundee
Who on that day the word of onset gave!
Like conquest would the Men of England see;
And her Foes find a like inglorious Grave.

25. ANTICIPATION.

October, 1803.

    Shout, for a mighty Victory is won!
On British ground the Invaders are laid low;
The breath of Heaven has drifted them like snow,
And left them lying in the silent sun,
Never to rise again!—the work is done.
Come forth, ye Old Men, now in peaceful show
And greet your Sons! drums beat, and trumpets blow!
Make merry, Wives! ye little Children stun
Your Grandame's ears with pleasure of your noise!
Clap, Infants, clap your hands! Divine must be
That triumph, when the very worst, the pain,
And even the prospect of our Brethren slain,
Hath something in it which the heart enjoys:—
In glory will they sleep and endless sanctity.

26.

November, 1803.

Another year!—another deadly blow!
Another mighty Empire overthrown!
And we are left, or shall be left, alone;
The last that dares to struggle with the Foe.
'Tis well! from this day forward we shall know
That in ourselves our safety must be sought;
That by our own right hands it must be wrought,
That we must stand unpropp'd, or be laid low.
O Dastard whom such foretaste doth not chear!
We shall exult, if They who rule the land
Be Men who hold its many blessings dear,
Wise, upright, valiant; not a venal Band,
Who are to judge of danger which they fear,
And honour which they do not understand.

NOTES TO THE FIRST VOLUME

NOTES.

NOTE I.

PAGE I (9).—*To the Daisy*. This Poem, and two others to the same Flower, which the Reader will find in the second Volume, were written in the year 1802; which is mentioned, because in some of the ideas, though not in the manner in which those ideas are connected, and likewise even in some of the expressions, they bear a striking resemblance to a Poem (lately published) of Mr. Montgomery, entitled, a Field Flower. This being said, Mr. Montgomery will not think any apology due to him; I cannot however help addressing him in the words of the Father of English Poets.

'Though it happe me to rehersin—
That ye han in your freshe song is saied,
Forberith me, and beth not ill apaied,
Sith that ye se I doe it in the honour
Of Love, and eke in service of the Flour.'

NOTE II.

PAGE 35 (43); line 13.—

".... persevering to the last,
From well to better."

'For Knightes ever should be persevering
To seek honour without feintise or slouth
Fro wele to better in all manner thing.'
              CHAUCER:—*The Floure and the Leafe.*

NOTE III.

PAGE 37 (45).—*The Horn of Egremont Castle.* This Story is a Cumberland tradition; I have heard it also related of the Hall of Hutton John an ancient residence of the Huddlestones, in a sequestered Valley upon the River Dacor.

NOTE IV.

PAGE 58 (64).—*The Seven Sisters.* The Story of this Poem is from the German of FREDERICA BRUN.

NOTE V.

Page 63 (71); line 6.—

    ".... that thy Boat
May rather seem
To brood on air," *&c. &c.*

   See Carver's Description of his Situation upon one of the Lakes of America.

NOTE VI.

PAGE 112 (120); line 8.—"Her tackling rich, and of apparel high."
From a passage in Skelton, which I cannot here insert, not having the
Book at hand.

NOTE VII.

PAGE 150 (158); line 11.—"Oh! for a single hour of that Dundee."
See an anecdote related in Mr. Scott's Border Minstrelsy.

NOTE VIII.

PAGE 152 (160); lines 13 and 14.—

  "Who are to judge of danger which they fear
And honour which they do not understand."

These two lines from Lord Brooke's Life of Sir Philip Sydney.

END OF THE FIRST VOLUME.

VOLUME II

POEMS WRITTEN DURING A TOUR IN SCOTLAND.

ROB ROY'S GRAVE.

The History of Rob Roy is sufficiently known; his Grave is near the head of Loch Ketterine, in one of those small Pin-fold-like Burial-grounds, of neglected and desolate appearance, which the Traveller meets with in the Highlands of Scotland.

A famous Man is Robin Hood,
The English Ballad-singer's joy!
And Scotland has a Thief as good,
An Outlaw of as daring mood,
She has her brave ROB ROY!
Then clear the weeds from off his Grave,
And let us chaunt a passing Stave
In honour of that Hero brave!

Heaven gave Rob Roy a dauntless heart,
And wondrous length and strength of arm: 10
Nor craved he more to quell his Foes,
Or keep his Friends from harm.

Yet was Rob Roy as *wise* as brave;
Forgive me if the phrase be strong;—

Poet worthy of Rob Roy
Must scorn a timid song.

Say, then, that he was wise as brave;
As wise in thought as bold in deed:
For in the principles of things
He sought his moral creed. 20

Said generous Rob, "What need of Books?
Burn all the Statutes and their shelves:
They stir us up against our Kind;
And worse, against Ourselves."

"We have a passion, make a law,
Too false to guide us or controul!
And for the law itself we fight
In bitterness of soul."

"And, puzzled, blinded thus, we lose
Distinctions that are plain and few: 30
These find I graven on my heart:
That tells me what to do."

"The Creatures see of flood and field,
And those that travel on the wind!
With them no strife can last; they live
In peace, and peace of mind."

"For why?—because the good old Rule
Sufficeth them, the simple Plan,
That they should take who have the power,
And they should keep who can." 40

"A lesson which is quickly learn'd,
A signal this which all can see!
Thus nothing here provokes the Strong
To wanton cruelty."

"All freakishness of mind is check'd;
He tam'd, who foolishly aspires;
While to the measure of his might
Each fashions his desires."

"All Kinds, and Creatures, stand and fall
By strength of prowess or of wit: 50
Tis God's appointment who must sway,
And who is to submit."

"Since then," said Robin, "right is plain,
And longest life is but a day;
To have my ends, maintain my rights,
I'll take the shortest way."

And thus among these rocks he liv'd,
Through summer's heat and winter's snow:
The Eagle, he was Lord above,
And Rob was Lord below. 60

So was it—*would*, at least, have been
But through untowardness of fate:
For Polity was then too strong;
He came an age too late,

Or shall we say an age too soon?
For, were the bold Man living *now*,

How might he flourish in his pride,
With buds on every bough!

Then rents and Factors, rights of chace,
Sheriffs, and Lairds and their domains 70
Would all have seem'd but paltry things,
Not worth a moment's pains.

Rob Roy had never linger'd here,
To these few meagre Vales confin'd;
But thought how wide the world, the times
How fairly to his mind!

And to his Sword he would have said,
"Do Thou my sovereign will enact
From land to land through half the earth!
Judge thou of law and fact!" 80

"Tis fit that we should do our part;
Becoming, that mankind should learn
That we are not to be surpass'd
In fatherly concern."

"Of old things all are over old,
Of good things none are good enough:—
We'll shew that we can help to frame
A world of other stuff."

"I, too, will have my Kings that take
From me the sign of life and death: 90
Kingdoms shall shift about, like clouds,
Obedient to my breath."

And, if the word had been fulfill'd,
As *might* have been, then, thought of joy!
France would have had her present Boast;
And we our brave Rob Roy!

Oh! say not so; compare them not;
I would not wrong thee, Champion brave!
Would wrong thee no where; least of all
Here standing by thy Grave. 100

For Thou, although with some wild thoughts,
Wild Chieftain of a Savage Clan!
Hadst this to boast of; thou didst love
The *liberty* of Man.

And, had it been thy lot to live
With us who now behold the light,
Thou would'st have nobly stirr'd thyself,
And battled for the Right.

For Robin was the poor Man's stay
The poor man's heart, the poor man's hand; 110
And all the oppress'd, who wanted strength,
Had Robin's to command.

Bear witness many a pensive sigh
Of thoughtful Herdsman when he strays
Alone upon Loch Veol's Heights,
And by Loch Lomond's Braes!

And, far and near, through vale and hill,
Are faces that attest the same;

And kindle, like a fire new stirr'd,
At sound of ROB ROY's name. 120

2. THE SOLITARY REAPER.

Behold her, single in the field,
Yon solitary Highland Lass!
Reaping and singing by herself;
Stop here, or gently pass!
Alone she cuts, and binds the grain,
And sings a melancholy strain;
O listen! for the Vale profound
Is overflowing with the sound.

No Nightingale did ever chaunt
So sweetly to reposing bands 10
Of Travellers in some shady haunt,
Among Arabian Sands:
No sweeter voice was ever heard
In spring-time from the Cuckoo-bird,
Breaking the silence of the seas
Among the farthest Hebrides.

Will no one tell me what she sings?
Perhaps the plaintive numbers flow
For old, unhappy, far-off things,
And battles long ago: 20
Or is it some more humble lay,
Familiar matter of today?

Some natural sorrow, loss, or pain,
That has been, and may be again!

Whate'er the theme, the Maiden sung
As if her song could have no ending;
I saw her singing at her work,
And o'er the sickle bending;
I listen'd till I had my fill;
And, as I mounted up the hill, 30
The music in my heart I bore,
Long after it was heard no more.

3. STEPPING WESTWARD.

While my Fellow-traveller and I were walking by the side
of Loch Ketterine, one fine evening after sun-set, in our
road to a Hut where in the course of our Tour we had been
hospitably entertained some weeks before, we met, in one
of the loneliest parts of that solitary region, two well
dressed Women, one of whom said to us, by way of
greeting, "What you are stepping westward?"

"*What you are stepping westward?*"—"*Yea.*"
—'Twould be a wildish destiny,
If we, who thus together roam
In a strange Land, and far from home,
Were in this place the guests of Chance:
Yet who would stop, or fear to advance,

Though home or shelter he had none,
With such a Sky to lead him on?

The dewy ground was dark and cold;
Behind, all gloomy to behold; 10
And stepping westward seem'd to be
A kind of *heavenly* destiny;
I liked the greeting; 'twas a sound
Of something without place or bound;
And seem'd to give me spiritual right
To travel through that region bright.

The voice was soft, and she who spake
Was walking by her native Lake:
The salutation had to me
The very sound of courtesy: 20
It's power was felt; and while my eye
Was fixed upon the glowing sky,
The echo of the voice enwrought
A human sweetness with the thought
Of travelling through the world that lay
Before me in my endless way.

4. *GLEN-ALMAIN*, OR THE NARROW GLEN

In this still place, remote from men,
Sleeps Ossian, in the NARROW GLEN;
In this still place, where murmurs on

But one meek Streamlet, only one:
He sang of battles, and the breath
Of stormy war, and violent death;
And should, methinks, when all was past,
Have rightfully been laid at last
Where rocks were sudely heap'd, and rent
As by a spirit turbulent; 10
Where sights were rough, and sounds were wild,
And every thing unreconciled;
In some complaining, dim retreat,
For fear and melancholy meet;
But this is calm; there cannot be
A more entire tranquillity.

    Does then the Bard sleep here indeed?
Or is it but a groundless creed?
What matters it? I blame them not
Whose Fancy in this lonely Spot 20
Was moved; and in this way express'd
Their notion of its perfect rest.
A Convent, even a hermit's Cell
Would break the silence of this Dell:
It is not quiet, is not ease;
But something deeper far than these:
The separation that is here
Is of the grave; and of austere
And happy feelings of the dead:
And, therefore, was it rightly said 30
That Ossian, last of all his race!
Lies buried in this lonely place.

5. THE MATRON OF JEDBOROUGH AND HER HUSBAND.

At Jedborough we went into private Lodgings for a few days; and the following Verses were called forth by the character, and domestic situation, of our Hostess.

Age! twine thy brows with fresh spring flowers!
And call a train of laughing Hours;
And bid them dance, and bid them sing;
And Thou, too, mingle in the Ring!
Take to thy heart a new delight;
If not, make merry in despite!
For there is one who scorns thy power.
—But dance! for under Jedborough Tower
There liveth in the prime of glee,
A Woman, whose years are seventy-three, 10
And She will dance and sing with thee!

Nay! start not at that Figure—there!
Him who is rooted to his chair!
Look at him—look again! for He
Hath long been of thy Family.
With legs that move not, if they can,
And useless arms, a Trunk of Man,
He sits, and with a vacant eye;
A Sight to make a Stranger sigh!
Deaf, drooping, that is now his doom: 20
His world is in this single room:
Is this a place for mirth and cheer?
Can merry-making enter here?

The joyous Woman is the Mate
Of Him in that forlorn estate!
He breathes a subterraneous damp,
But bright as Vesper shines her lamp:
He is as mute as Jedborough Tower;
She jocund as it was of yore,
With all its bravery on; in times, 30
When, all alive with merry chimes,
Upon a sun-bright morn of May,
It rouz'd the Vale to Holiday.

I praise thee, Matron! and thy due
Is praise; heroic praise, and true!
With admiration I behold
Thy gladness unsubdued and bold:
Thy looks, thy gestures, all present
The picture of a life well-spent:
This do I see; and something more; 40
A strength unthought of heretofore!
Delighted am I for thy sake;
And yet a higher joy partake.
Our Human-nature throws away
It's second Twilight, and looks gay:
A Land of promise and of pride
Unfolding, wide as life is wide.

Ah! see her helpless Charge! enclos'd
Within himself, as seems; compos'd;
To fear of loss, and hope of gain, 50
The strife of happiness and pain,
Utterly dead! yet, in the guise
Of little Infants, when their eyes

Begin to follow to and fro
The persons that before them go,
He tracks her motions, quick or slow.
Her buoyant Spirit can prevail
Where common cheerfulness would fail:
She strikes upon him with the heat
Of July Suns; he feels it sweet; 60
An animal delight though dim!
'Tis all that now remains for him!

I look'd, I scann'd her o'er and o'er;
The more I look'd I wonder'd more:
When suddenly I seem'd to espy
A trouble in her strong black eye;
A remnant of uneasy light,
A flash of something over-bright!
And soon she made this matter plain;
And told me, in a thoughtful strain, 70
That she had borne a heavy yoke,
Been stricken by a twofold stroke;
Ill health of body; and had pin'd
Beneath worse ailments of the mind.

So be it! but let praise ascend
To Him who is our Lord and Friend!
Who from disease and suffering
Hath call'd for thee a second Spring;
Repaid thee for that sore distress
By no untimely joyousness; 80
Which makes of thine a blissful state;
And cheers thy melancholy Mate!

6. TO A HIGHLAND GIRL.

(At Inversneyde, upon Loch Lomond.)

 Sweet Highland Girl, a very shower
Of beauty is thy earthly dower!
Twice seven consenting years have shed
Their utmost bounty on thy head:
And these gray Rocks; this household Lawn;
These Trees, a veil just half withdrawn;
This fall of water, that doth make
A murmur near the silent Lake;
This little Bay, a quiet Road
That holds in shelter thy Abode; 10
In truth together ye do seem
Like something fashion'd in a dream;

 Such Forms as from their covert peep
When earthly cares are laid asleep!
Yet, dream and vision as thou art,
I bless thee with a human heart:
God shield thee to thy latest years!
I neither know thee nor thy peers;
And yet my eyes are fill'd with tears.

 With earnest feeling I shall pray 20
For thee when I am far away:
For never saw I mien, or face,
In which more plainly I could trace
Benignity and home-bred sense
Ripening in perfect innocence.

Here, scatter'd like a random seed,
Remote from men, Thou dost not need
The embarrass'd look of shy distress,
And maidenly shamefacedness:

Thou wear'st upon thy forehead clear 30
The freedom of a Mountaineer.
A face with gladness overspread!
Sweet looks, by human kindness bred!
And seemliness complete, that sways
Thy courtesies, about thee plays;
With no restraint, but such as springs
From quick and eager visitings
Of thoughts, that lie beyond the reach
Of thy few words of English speech:
A bondage sweetly brook'd, a strife 40
That gives thy gestures grace and life!
So have I, not unmov'd in mind,
Seen birds of tempest-loving kind,
Thus beating up against the wind.

What hand but would a garland cull
For thee who art so beautiful?
O happy pleasure! here to dwell
Beside thee in some heathy dell;
Adopt your homely ways and dress,
A Shepherd, thou a Shepherdess! 50
But I could frame a wish for thee
More like a grave reality:
Thou art to me but as a wave
Of the wild sea; and I would have
Some claim upon thee, if I could,

Though but of common neighbourhood.
What joy to hear thee, and to see!
Thy elder Brother I would be,
Thy Father, any thing to thee!

Now thanks to Heaven! that of its grace 60
Hath led me to this lonely place.
Joy have I had; and going hence
I bear away my recompence.
In spots like these it is we prize
Our Memory, feel that she hath eyes:
Then, why should I be loth to stir?
I feel this place was made for her;
To give new pleasure like the past,
Continued long as life shall last.
Nor am I loth, though pleased at heart, 70
Sweet Highland Girl! from Thee to part;
For I, methinks, till I grow old,
As fair before me shall behold,
As I do now, the Cabin small,
The Lake, the Bay, the Waterfall;
And Thee, the Spirit of them all!

7. SONNET.

(Composed at —— Castle.)

Degenerate Douglas! oh, the unworthy Lord!
Whom mere despite of heart could so far please,
And love of havoc (for with such disease
Fame taxes him) that he could send forth word
To level with the dust a noble horde,
A brotherhood of venerable Trees,
Leaving an ancient Dome, and Towers like these,
Beggared and outraged!—Many hearts deplor'd
The fate of those old Trees; and oft with pain
The Traveller, at this day, will stop and gaze
On wrongs, which Nature scarcely seems to heed:
For shelter'd places, bosoms, nooks and bays,
And the pure mountains, and the gentle Tweed,
And the green silent pastures, yet remain.

8. ADDRESS TO THE SONS OF BURNS
after visiting their Father's Grave (August 14th, 1803.)

Ye now are panting up life's hill!
'Tis twilight time of good and ill,
And more than common strength and skill
    Must ye display
If ye would give the better will
    Its lawful sway.

Strong bodied if ye be to bear
Intemperance with less harm, beware!
But if your Father's wit ye share,
    Then, then indeed, 10
Ye Sons of Burns! for watchful care
    There will be need.

For honest men delight will take
To shew you favor for his sake,
Will flatter you; and Fool and Rake
    Your steps pursue:
And of your Father's name will make
    A snare for you.

Let no mean hope your souls enslave;
Be independent, generous, brave! 20
Your Father such example gave,
    And such revere!
But be admonish'd by his Grave,
    And think, and fear!

9. YARROW UNVISITED.

(See the various Poems the scene of which is laid upon the
Banks of the Yarrow; in particular, the exquisite Ballad
of Hamilton, beginning:
  "Busk ye, busk ye my bonny, bonny Bride,
  Busk ye, busk ye my winsome Marrow!"—)

From Stirling Castle we had seen
The mazy Forth unravell'd;
Had trod the banks of Clyde, and Tay,
And with the Tweed had travell'd;
And, when we came to Clovenford,
Then said my '*winsome Marrow*',
"Whate'er betide, we'll turn aside,
And see the Braes of Yarrow."

"Let Yarrow Folk, *frae* Selkirk Town,
Who have been buying, selling,   10
Go back to Yarrow, 'tis their own,
Each Maiden to her Dwelling!
On Yarrow's Banks let herons feed,
Hares couch, and rabbits burrow!
But we will downwards with the Tweed,
Nor turn aside to Yarrow."

"There's Galla Water, Leader Haughs,
Both lying right before us;
And Dryborough, where with chiming Tweed
The Lintwhites sing in chorus;   20
There's pleasant Tiviot Dale, a land
Made blithe with plough and harrow;
Why throw away a needful day
To go in search of Yarrow?"

"What's Yarrow but a River bare
That glides the dark hills under?
There are a thousand such elsewhere
As worthy of your wonder."
—Strange words they seem'd of slight and scorn;

My True-love sigh'd for sorrow; 30
And look'd me in the face, to think
I thus could speak of Yarrow!

"Oh! green," said I, "are Yarrow's Holms,
And sweet is Yarrow flowing!
Fair hangs the apple frae the rock [1],
But we will leave it growing.
O'er hilly path, and open Strath,
We'll wander Scotland thorough;
But, though so near, we will not turn
Into the Dale of Yarrow." 40

[Footnote 1: See Hamilton's Ballad as above.]

"Let Beeves and home-bred Kine partake
The sweets of Burn-mill meadow;
The Swan on still St. Mary's Lake
Float double, Swan and Shadow!
We will not see them; will not go,
Today, nor yet tomorrow;
Enough if in our hearts we know,
There's such a place as Yarrow."

"Be Yarrow Stream unseen, unknown!
It must, or we shall rue it: 50
We have a vision of our own;
Ah! why should we undo it?
The treasured dreams of times long past
We'll keep them, winsome Marrow!
For when we're there although 'tis fair
'Twill be another Yarrow!"

"If Care with freezing years should come,
And wandering seem but folly,
Should we be loth to stir from home,
And yet be melancholy; 60
Should life be dull, and spirits low,
'Twill soothe us in our sorrow
That earth has something yet to show,
The bonny Holms of Yarrow!"

MOODS OF MY OWN MIND.

1. TO A BUTTERFLY.

Stay near me—do not take thy flight!
A little longer stay in sight!
Much converse do I find in Thee,
Historian of my Infancy!
Float near me; do not yet depart!
Dead times revive in thee:
Thou bring'st, gay Creature as thou art!
A solemn image to my heart,
My Father's Family!

Oh! pleasant, pleasant were the days,
The time, when in our childish plays
My sister Emmeline and I
Together chaced the Butterfly!
A very hunter did I rush
Upon the prey:—with leaps and springs
I follow'd on from brake to bush;
But She, God love her! feared to brush
The dust from off its wings.

2.

The Sun has long been set:
The Stars are out by twos and threes;
The little Birds are piping yet
Among the bushes and trees;
There's a Cuckoo, and one or two thrushes;
And a noise of wind that rushes,
With a noise of water that gushes;
And the Cuckoo's sovereign cry
Fills all the hollow of the sky!

Who would go "parading" 10
In London, and "masquerading,"
On such a night of June?
With that beautiful soft half-moon,
And all these innocent blisses,
On such a night as this is!

3.

O Nightingale! thou surely art
A Creature of a fiery heart—
These notes of thine they pierce, and pierce;
Tumultuous harmony and fierce!
Thou sing'st as if the God of wine
Had help'd thee to a Valentine;
A song in mockery and despite
Of shades, and dews, and silent Night,

And steady bliss, and all the Loves
Now sleeping in these peaceful groves! 10

I heard a Stockdove sing or say
His homely tale, this very day.
His voice was buried among trees,
Yet to be come at by the breeze:
He did not cease; but coo'd—and coo'd;
And somewhat pensively he woo'd:
He sang of love with quiet blending,
Slow to begin, and never ending;
Of serious faith, and inward glee;
That was the Song, the Song for me! 20

4.

My heart leaps up when I behold
    A Rainbow in the sky:
So was it when my life began;
So is it now I am a Man;
So be it when I shall grow old,
    Or let me die!
The Child is Father of the Man;
And I could wish my days to be
Bound each to each by natural piety.

5. WRITTEN IN MARCH,
WHILE RESTING ON THE BRIDGE AT THE FOOT OF BROTHER'S WATER.

The cook is crowing,
The stream is flowing,
The small birds twitter,
The lake doth glitter,
The green field sleeps in the sun;
The oldest and youngest
Are at work with the strongest;
The cattle are grazing,
Their heads never raising;
There are forty feeding like one! 10
Like an army defeated
The Snow hath retreated,
And now doth fare ill
On the top of the bare hill;
The Plough-boy is whooping—anon—anon:
There's joy in the mountains;
There's life in the fountains;
Small clouds are sailing,
Blue sky prevailing;
The rain is over and gone! 20

6. THE SMALL CELANDINE.
Common Pilewort.

There is a Flower, the Lesser Celandine,
That shrinks, like many more, from cold and rain;
And, the first moment that the sun may shine,
Bright as the sun itself, 'tis out again!

When hailstones have been falling swarm on swarm,
Or blasts the green field and the trees distress'd,
Oft have I seen it muffled up from harm,
In close self-shelter, like a Thing at rest.

But lately, one rough day, this Flower I pass'd,
And recognized it, though an alter'd Form, 10
Now standing forth an offering to the Blast,
And buffetted at will by Rain and Storm,

I stopp'd, and said with inly muttered voice,
"It doth not love the shower, nor seek the cold:
This neither is its courage nor its choice,
But its necessity in being old."

The sunshine may not bless it, nor the dew;
It cannot help itself in its decay;
Stiff in its members, wither'd, changed of hue.
And, in my spleen, I smiled that it was grey. 20

To be a Prodigal's Favorite—then, worse truth,
A Miser's Pensioner—behold our lot!
O Man! that from thy fair and shining youth
Age might but take the things Youth needed not!

7.

I wandered lonely as a Cloud
That floats on high o'er Vales and Hills,
When all at once I saw a crowd
A host of dancing Daffodills;
Along the Lake, beneath the trees,
Ten thousand dancing in the breeze.

The waves beside them danced, but they
Outdid the sparkling waves in glee:—
A Poet could not but be gay
In such a laughing company: 10
I gaz'd—and gaz'd—but little thought
What wealth the shew to me had brought:

For oft when on my couch I lie
In vacant or in pensive mood,
They flash upon that inward eye
Which is the bliss of solitude,
And then my heart with pleasure fills,
And dances with the Daffodils.

8.

Who fancied what a pretty sight
This Rock would be if edged around
With living Snowdrops? circlet bright!
How glorious to this Orchard ground!

Who loved the little Rock, and set
Upon its Head this Coronet?

Was it the humour of a Child?
Or rather of some love-sick Maid,
Whose brows, the day that she was styled
The Shepherd Queen, were thus arrayed?
Of Man mature, or Matron sage?
Or old Man toying with his age?

I ask'd—'twas whisper'd, The device
To each or all might well belong.
It is the Spirit of Paradise
That prompts such work, a Spirit strong,
That gives to all the self-same bent
Where life is wise and innocent.

9. THE SPARROW'S NEST.

Look, five blue eggs are gleaming there!
Few visions have I seen more fair,
Nor many prospects of delight
More pleasing than that simple sight!
I started seeming to espy
The home and shelter'd bed,
The Sparrow's dwelling, which, hard by
My Father's House, in wet or dry,
My Sister Emmeline and I
    Together visited. 10

She look'd at it as if she fear'd it;
Still wishing, dreading to be near it:
Such heart was in her, being then
A little Prattler among men.
The Blessing of my later years
Was with me when a Boy;
She gave me eyes, she gave me ears;
And humble cares, and delicate fears;
A heart, the fountain of sweet tears;
    And love, and thought, and joy. 20

10. GIPSIES.

Yet are they here?—the same unbroken knot
Of human Beings, in the self-same spot!
    Men, Women, Children, yea the frame
    Of the whole Spectacle the same!
Only their fire seems bolder, yielding light:
Now deep and red, the colouring of night;
    That on their Gipsy-faces falls,
    Their bed of straw and blanket-walls.
—Twelve hours, twelve bounteous hours, are gone while I
Have been a Traveller under open sky, 10
    Much witnessing of change and chear,
    Yet as I left I find them here!

    The weary Sun betook himself to rest.
—Then issued Vesper from the fulgent West,
    Outshining like a visible God

The glorious path in which he trod.
And now, ascending, after one dark hour,
And one night's diminution of her power,
  Behold the mighty Moon! this way
  She looks as if at them—but they 20
Regard not her:—oh better wrong and strife,
Better vain deeds or evil than such life!
  The silent Heavens have goings on;
  The stars have tasks—but these have none.

11. TO THE CUCKOO.

  O blithe New-comer! I have heard,
I hear thee and rejoice:
O Cuckoo! shall I call thee Bird,
Or but a wandering Voice?

  While I am lying on the grass,
I hear thy restless shout:
From hill to hill it seems to pass,
About, and all about!

  To me, no Babbler with a tale
Of sunshine and of flowers, 10
Thou tellest, Cuckoo! in the vale
Of visionary hours.

  Thrice welcome, Darling of the Spring!
Even yet thou art to me

No Bird; but an invisible Thing,
A voice, a mystery.

The same whom in my School-boy days
I listen'd to; that Cry
Which made me look a thousand ways;
In bush, and tree, and sky. 20

To seek thee did I often rove
Through woods and on the green;
And thou wert still a hope, a love;
Still long'd for, never seen!

And I can listen to thee yet;
Can lie upon the plain.
And listen, till I do beget
That golden time again.

O blessed Bird! the earth we pace
Again appears to be 30
An unsubstantial, faery place;
That is fit home for Thee!

12. TO A BUTTERFLY.

I've watch'd you now a full half hour,
Self-pois'd upon that yellow flower;
And, little Butterfly! indeed
I know not if you sleep, or feed.
How motionless! not frozen seas
More motionless! and then
What joy awaits you, when the breeze
Hath found you out among the trees,
    And calls you forth again!

    This plot of Orchard-ground is ours; 10
My trees they are, my Sister's flowers;
Stop here whenever you are weary,
And rest as in a sanctuary!
Come often to us, fear no wrong;
Sit near us on the bough!
We'll talk of sunshine and of song;
And summer days, when we were young,
Sweet childish days, that were as long
    As twenty days are now!

13.

It is no Spirit who from Heaven hath flown,
    And is descending on his embassy;
    Nor Traveller gone from Earth the Heavens to espy!
'Tis Hesperus—there he stands with glittering crown,
First admonition that the sun is down!

For yet it is broad day-light: clouds pass by;
A few are near him still—and now the sky,
He hath it to himself—'tis all his own.
O most ambitious Star! an inquest wrought
Within me when I recognised thy light;
A moment I was startled at the sight:
And, while I gazed, there came to me a thought
That I might step beyond my natural race
As thou seem'st now to do; might one day trace
Some ground not mine; and, strong her strength above,
My Soul, an Apparition in the place,
Tread there, with steps that no one shall reprove!

THE BLIND HIGHLAND BOY; WITH OTHER POEMS.

THE BLIND HIGHLAND BOY.
(A Tale told by the Fire-side.)

Now we are tired of boisterous joy,
We've romp'd enough, my little Boy!
Jane hangs her head upon my breast,
And you shall bring your Stool and rest,
   This corner is your own.

  There! take your seat, and let me see
That you can listen quietly;
And as I promised I will tell
That strange adventure which befel
   A poor blind Highland Boy. 10

  A *Highland* Boy!—why call him so?
Because, my Darlings, ye must know,
In land where many a mountain towers,
Far higher hills than these of ours!
   He from his birth had liv'd.

  He ne'er had seen one earthly sight;
The sun, the day; the stars, the night;
Or tree, or butterfly, or flower,
Or fish in stream, or bird in bower,
   Or woman, man, or child. 20

And yet he neither drooped nor pined,
Nor had a melancholy mind;
For God took pity on the Boy,
And was his friend; and gave him joy
 Of which we nothing know.

His Mother, too, no doubt, above
Her other Children him did love:
For, was she here, or was she there,
She thought of him with constant care,
 And more than Mother's love. 30

And proud she was of heart, when clad
In crimson stockings, tartan plaid,
And bonnet with a feather gay,
To Kirk he on the sabbath day
 Went hand in hand with her.

A Dog, too, had he; not for need,
But one to play with and to feed;
Which would have led him, if bereft
Of company or friends, and left
 Without a better guide. 40

And then the bagpipes he could blow;
And thus from house to house would go,
And all were pleas'd to hear and see;
For none made sweeter melody
 Than did the poor blind Boy.

Yet he had many a restless dream;
Both when he heard the Eagles scream,
And when he heard the torrents roar,

And heard the water beat the shore
    Near which their Cottage stood. 50

    Beside a lake their Cottage stood,
Not small like ours, a peaceful flood;
But one of mighty size, and strange;
That, rough or smooth, is full of change,
    And stirring in its bed.

    For to this Lake, by night and day,
The great Sea-water finds its way
Through long, long windings of the hills;
And drinks up all the pretty rills
    And rivers large and strong: 60

    Then hurries back the road it came—
Returns, on errand still the same;
This did it when the earth was new;
And this for evermore will do,
    As long as earth shall last.

    And, with the coming of the Tide,
Come Boats and Ships, that sweetly ride,
Between the woods and lofty rocks;
And to the Shepherds with their Flocks
    Bring tales of distant Lands. 70

    And of those tales, whate'er they were,
The blind Boy always had his share;
Whether of mighty Towns, or Vales
With warmer suns and softer gales,
    Or wonders of the Deep.

Yet more it pleased him, more it stirr'd,
When from the water-side he heard
The shouting, and the jolly cheers,
The bustle of the mariners
   In stillness or in storm. 80

But what do his desires avail?
For He must never handle sail;
Nor mount the mast, nor row, nor float
In Sailor's ship or Fisher's boat
   Upon the rocking waves.

His Mother often thought, and said,
What sin would be upon her head
If she should suffer this: "My Son,
Whate'er you do, leave this undone;
   The danger is so great." 90

Thus lived he by Loch Levin's side
Still sounding with the sounding tide,
And heard the billows leap and dance,
Without a shadow of mischance,
   Till he was ten years old.

When one day (and now mark me well,
You soon shall know how this befel)
He's in a vessel of his own,
On the swift water hurrying down
   Towards the mighty Sea. 100

In such a vessel ne'er before
Did human Creature leave the shore:
If this or that way he should stir,

Woe to the poor blind Mariner!
  For death will be his doom.

  Strong is the current; but be mild,
Ye waves, and spare the helpless Child!
If ye in anger fret or chafe,
A Bee-hive would be ship as safe
  As that in which he sails. 110

  But say, what was it? Thought of fear!
Well may ye tremble when ye hear!
—A Household Tub, like one of those
Which women use to wash their clothes,
  This carried the blind Boy.

  Close to the water he had found
This Vessel, push'd it from dry ground,
Went into it; and, without dread,
Following the fancies in his head,
  He paddled up and down. 120

  A while he stood upon his feet;
He felt the motion—took his seat;
And dallied thus, till from the shore
The tide retreating more and more
  Had suck'd, and suck'd him in.

  And there he is in face of Heaven!
How rapidly the Child is driven!
The fourth part of a mile I ween
He thus had gone, ere he was seen
  By any human eye. 130

But when he was first seen, oh me!
What shrieking and what misery!
For many saw; among the rest
His Mother, she who loved him best,
    She saw her poor blind Boy.

    But for the Child, the sightless Boy,
It is the triumph of his joy!
The bravest Traveller in balloon,
Mounting as if to reach the moon,
    Was never half so bless'd. 140

    And let him, let him go his way,
Alone, and innocent, and gay!
For, if good Angels love to wait
On the forlorn unfortunate,
    This Child will take no harm.

    But now the passionate lament,
Which from the crowd on shore was sent,
The cries which broke from old and young
In Gaelic, or the English tongue,
    Are stifled—all is still. 150

    And quickly with a silent crew
A Boat is ready to pursue;
And from the shore their course they take,
And swiftly down the running Lake
    They follow the blind Boy.

    With sound the least that can be made
They follow, more and more afraid,
More cautious as they draw more near;

But in his darkness he can hear,
    And guesses their intent. 160

    "*Lei-gha—Lei-gha*"—then did he cry
"*Lei-gha—Lei-gha*"—most eagerly;
Thus did he cry, and thus did pray,
And what he meant was, "Keep away,
    And leave me to myself!"

    Alas! and when he felt their hands—
You've often heard of magic Wands,
That with a motion overthrow
A palace of the proudest shew,
    Or melt it into air. 170

    So all his dreams, that inward light
With which his soul had shone so bright,
All vanish'd;—'twas a heartfelt cross
To him, a heavy, bitter loss,
    As he had ever known.

    But hark! a gratulating voice
With which the very hills rejoice:
'Tis from the crowd, who tremblingly
Had watch'd the event, and now can see
    That he is safe at last. 180

    And then, when he was brought to land,
Full sure they were a happy band,
Which gathering round did on the banks
Of that great Water give God thanks,
    And welcom'd the poor Child.

And in the general joy of heart
The blind Boy's little Dog took part;
He leapt about, and oft did kiss
His master's hands in sign of bliss,
    With sound like lamentation. 190

But most of all, his Mother dear,
She who had fainted with her fear,
Rejoiced when waking she espies
The Child; when she can trust her eyes,
    And touches the blind Boy.

She led him home, and wept amain,
When he was in the house again:
Tears flow'd in torrents from her eyes,
She could not blame him, or chastise:
    She was too happy far. 200

Thus, after he had fondly braved
The perilous Deep, the Boy was saved;
And, though his fancies had been wild,
Yet he was pleased, and reconciled
    To live in peace on shore.

THE GREEN LINNET.

The May is come again:—how sweet
To sit upon my Orchard-seat!
And Birds and Flowers once more to greet,
   My last year's Friends together:
My thoughts they all by turns employ;
A whispering Leaf is now my joy,
And then a Bird will be the toy
   That doth my fancy tether.

One have I mark'd, the happiest Guest
In all this covert of the blest: 10
Hail to Thee, far above the rest
   In joy of voice and pinion,
Thou, Linnet! in thy green array,
Presiding Spirit here to-day,
Dost lead the revels of the May,
   And this is thy dominion.

While Birds, and Butterflies, and Flowers
Make all one Band of Paramours,
Thou, ranging up and down the bowers,
   Art sole in thy employment; 20
A Life, a Presence like the Air,
Scattering thy gladness without care,
Too bless'd with any one to pair,
   Thyself thy own enjoyment.

Upon yon tuft of hazel trees,
That twinkle to the gusty breeze,
Behold him perch'd in ecstasies,
   Yet seeming still to hover;

There! where the flutter of his wings
Upon his back and body flings 30
Shadows and sunny glimmerings,
    That cover him all over.

    While thus before my eyes he gleams,
A Brother of the Leaves he seems;
When in a moment forth he teems
    His little song in gushes:
As if it pleas'd him to disdain
And mock the Form which he did feign,
While he was dancing with the train
    Of Leaves among the bushes. 40

TO A YOUNG LADY,
Who had been reproached for taking long Walks in the Country.

    Dear Child of Nature, let them rail!
—There is a nest in a green dale,
A harbour and a hold,
Where thou a Wife and Friend, shalt see
Thy own delightful days, and be
A light to young and old.

    There, healthy as a Shepherd-boy,
As if thy heritage were joy,

And pleasure were thy trade,
Thou, while thy Babes around thee cling,
Shalt shew us how divine a thing
A Woman may be made.

   Thy thoughts and feelings shall not die,
Nor leave thee, when grey hairs are nigh,
A melancholy slave
But an old age, alive and bright,
And lovely as a Lapland night,
Shall lead thee to thy grave.
"*—Pleasure is spread through the earth*
In stray gifts to be claim'd by whoever shall find."

* * * * *

   By their floating Mill,
  Which lies dead and still,
Behold yon Prisoners three!
The Miller with two Dames, on the breast of the Thames;
The Platform is small, but there's room for them all;
And they're dancing merrily.

   From the shore come the notes
  To their Mill where it floats,
To their House and their Mill tether'd fast;
To the small wooden isle where their work to beguile 10
They from morning to even take whatever is given;—
And many a blithe day they have past.

In sight of the Spires
  All alive with the fires
Of the Sun going down to his rest,
In the broad open eye of the solitary sky,
They dance,—there are three, as jocund as free,
While they dance on the calm river's breast.

  Man and Maidens wheel,
    They themselves make the Reel, 20
And their Music's a prey which they seize;
It plays not for them,—what matter! 'tis their's;
And if they had care it has scattered their cares,
While they dance, crying, "Long as ye please!"

  They dance not for me,
    Yet mine is their glee!
Thus pleasure is spread through the earth
In stray gifts to be claim'd by whoever shall find;
Thus a rich loving-kindness, redundantly kind,
Moves all nature to gladness and mirth. 30

  The Showers of the Spring
    Rouze the Birds and they sing;
If the Wind do but stir for his proper delight,
Each Leaf, that and this, his neighbour will kiss,
Each Wave, one and t'other, speeds after his Brother;
They are happy, for that is their right!

STAR GAZERS.

What crowd is this? what have we here! we must not pass it by;
A Telescope upon its frame, and pointed to the sky:
Long is it as a Barber's Poll, or Mast of little Boat,
Some little Pleasure-Skiff, that doth on Thames's waters float.

The Show-man chuses well his place, 'tis Leicester's busy Square;
And he's as happy in his night, for the heavens are blue and fair;
Calm, though impatient is the Crowd; Each is ready with the fee,
And envies him that's looking—what an insight must it be!

Yet, Show-man, where can lie the cause? Shall thy Implement have

    blame,
A Boaster, that when he is tried, fails, and is put to shame? 10
Or is it good as others are, and be their eyes in fault?
Their eyes, or minds? or, finally, is this resplendent Vault?

Is nothing of that radiant pomp so good as we have here?
Or gives a thing but small delight that never can be dear?
The silver Moon with all her Vales, and Hills of mightiest fame,
Do they betray us when they're seen? and are they but a name?

Or is it rather that Conceit rapacious is and strong,
And bounty never yields so much but it seems to do her wrong?
Or is it, that when human Souls a journey long have had,
And are returned into themselves, they cannot but be sad? 20

Or must we be constrain'd to think that these Spectators rude,
Poor in estate, of manners base, men of the multitude,
Have souls which never yet have ris'n, and therefore prostrate lie?
No, no, this cannot be—Men thirst for power and majesty!

Does, then, a deep and earnest thought the blissful mind employ
Of him who gazes, or has gazed? a grave and steady joy,
That doth reject all shew of pride, admits no outward sign,
Because not of this noisy world, but silent and divine!

Whatever be the cause, 'tis sure that they who pry & pore
Seem to meet with little gain, seem less happy than before: 30
One after One they take their turns, nor have I one espied
That doth not slackly go away, as if dissatisfied.

POWER OF MUSIC.

An Orpheus! An Orpheus!—yes, Faith may grow bold,
And take to herself all the wonders of old;—
Near the stately Pantheon you'll meet with the same,
In the street that from Oxford hath borrowed its name.

His station is there;—and he works on the crowd,
He sways them with harmony merry and loud;
He fills with his power all their hearts to the brim—
Was aught ever heard like his fiddle and him!

What an eager assembly! what an empire is this!
The weary have life and the hungry have bliss; 10
The mourner is cheared, and the anxious have rest;
And the guilt-burthened Soul is no longer opprest.

As the Moon brightens round her the clouds of the night,
So he where he stands is a center of light;

It gleams on the face, there, of dusky-faced Jack,
And the pale-visaged Baker's, with basket on back.

That errand-bound 'Prentice was passing in haste—
What matter! he's caught—and his time runs to waste—
The News-man is stopped, though he stops on the fret,
And the half-breathless Lamp-lighter he's in the net! 20

The Porter sits down on the weight which he bore;
The Lass with her barrow wheels hither her store;—
If a Thief could be here he might pilfer at ease;
She sees the Musician, 'tis all that she sees!

He stands, back'd by the Wall;—he abates not his din;
His hat gives him vigour, with boons dropping in,
From the Old and the Young, from the Poorest; and there!
The one-pennied Boy has his penny to spare.

O blest are the Hearers and proud be the Hand
Of the pleasure it spreads through so thankful a Band; 30
I am glad for him, blind as he is!—all the while
If they speak 'tis to praise, and they praise with a smile.

That tall Man, a Giant in bulk and in height,
Not an inch of his body is free from delight;
Can he keep himself still, if he would? oh, not he!
The music stirs in him like wind through a tree.

There's a Cripple who leans on his Crutch; like a Tower
That long has lean'd forward, leans hour after hour!—
Mother, whose Spirit in fetters is bound,
While she dandles the babe in her arms to the sound. 40

Now, Coaches and Chariots, roar on like a stream;
Here are twenty souls happy as Souls in a dream:
They are deaf to your murmurs—they care not for you,
Nor what ye are flying, or what ye pursue!

TO THE DAISY.

The two following Poems were overflowings of the mind in
composing the one which stands first in the first Volume.

With little here to do or see
Of things that in the great world be,
Sweet Daisy! oft I talk to thee,
    For thou art worthy,
Thou unassuming Common-place
Of Nature, with that homely face,
And yet with something of a grace,
    Which Love makes for thee!

Oft do I sit by thee at ease,
And weave a web of similies, 10
Loose types of Things through all degrees,
    Thoughts of thy raising:
And many a fond and idle name
I give to thee, for praise or blame,
As is the humour of the game,
    While I am gazing.

A Nun demure of lowly port,
Or sprightly Maiden of Love's Court,
In thy simplicity the sport
    Of all temptations; 20
A Queen in crown of rubies drest,
A Starveling in a scanty vest,
Are all, as seem to suit thee best,
    Thy appellations.

    A little Cyclops, with one eye
Staring to threaten and defy,
That thought comes next—and instantly
    The freak is over,
The shape will vanish, and behold!
A silver Shield with boss of gold, 30
That spreads itself, some Faery bold
    In fight to cover.

    I see thee glittering from afar;—
And then thou art a pretty Star,
Not quite so fair as many are
    In heaven above thee!
Yet, like a star, with glittering crest,
Self-poised in air thou seem'st to rest;—
May peace come never to his nest,
    Who shall reprove thee! 40

    Sweet Flower! for by that name at last,
When all my reveries are past,
I call thee, and to that cleave fast,
    Sweet silent Creature!
That breath'st with me in sun and air,
Do thou, as thou art wont, repair

My heart with gladness, and a share
   Of thy meek nature!

TO THE SAME FLOWER.

  Bright Flower, whose home is every where!
A Pilgrim bold in Nature's care,
And all the long year through the heir
   Of joy or sorrow,
Methinks that there abides in thee
Some concord with humanity,
Given to no other Flower I see
   The forest thorough!

  Is it that Man is soon deprest?
A thoughtless Thing! who, once unblest, 10
Does little on his memory rest,
   Or on his reason,
And Thou would'st teach him how to find
A shelter under every wind.
A hope for times that are unkind
   And every season?

  Thou wander'st the wide world about,
Uncheck'd by pride or scrupulous doubt,
With friends to greet thee, or without,
   Yet pleased and willing; 20
Meek, yielding to the occasion's call,
And all things suffering from all,

Thy function apostolical
  In peace fulfilling.

INCIDENT,

Characteristic of a favourite Dog, which belonged
to a Friend of the Author.

On his morning rounds the Master
Goes to learn how all things fare;
Searches pasture after pasture,
Sheep and Cattle eyes with care;
And, for silence or for talk,
He hath Comrades in his walk;
Four Dogs, each pair of different breed,
Distinguished two for scent, and two for speed.

See, a Hare before him started!
—Off they fly in earnest chace; 10
Every Dog is eager-hearted,
All the four are in the race!
And the Hare whom they pursue
Hath an instinct what to do;
Her hope is near: no turn she makes;
But, like an arrow, to the River takes.

Deep the River was, and crusted
Thinly by a one night's frost;
But the nimble Hare hath trusted

To the ice, and safely crost; 20
She hath crost, and without heed
All are following at full speed,
When, lo! the ice, so thinly spread,
Breaks—and the Greyhound, DART, is over head!

Better fate have PRINCE and SWALLOW—
See them cleaving to the sport!
Music has no heart to follow,
Little Music, she stops short.
She hath neither wish nor heart.
Her's is now another part: 30
A loving Creature she, and brave!
And doth her best her struggling Friend to save.

From the brink her paws she stretches,
Very hands as you would say!
And afflicting moans she fetches,
As he breaks the ice away.
For herself she hath no fears,
Him alone she sees and hears,
Makes efforts and complainings; nor gives o'er
Until her Fellow sunk, and reappear'd no more. 40

TRIBUTE TO THE MEMORY OF THE SAME DOG.

Lie here sequester'd:—be this little mound
For ever thine, and be it holy ground!
Lie here, without a record of thy worth,
Beneath the covering of the common earth!
It is not from unwillingness to praise,
Or want of love, that here no Stone we raise;
More thou deserv'st; but *this* Man gives to Man,
Brother to Brother, *this* is all we can.
Yet they to whom thy virtues made thee dear
Shall find thee through all changes of the year: 10
This Oak points out thy grave; the silent Tree
Will gladly stand a monument of thee.

I pray'd for thee, and that thy end were past;
And willingly have laid thee here at last:
For thou hadst liv'd, till every thing that chears
In thee had yielded to the weight of years;
Extreme old age had wasted thee away,
And left thee but a glimmering of the day;
Thy ears were deaf; and feeble were thy knees,—
saw thee stagger in the summer breeze, 20
Too weak to stand against its sportive breath,
And ready for the gentlest stroke of death.
It came, and we were glad; yet tears were shed;
Both Man and Woman wept when Thou wert dead;
Not only for a thousand thoughts that were,
Old household thoughts, in which thou hadst thy share;
But for some precious boons vouchsafed to thee,
Found scarcely any where in like degree!

For love, that comes to all; the holy sense,
Best gift of God, in thee was most intense; 30
A chain of heart, a feeling of the mind,
A tender sympathy, which did thee bind
Not only to us Men, but to thy Kind:
Yea, for thy Fellow-brutes in thee we saw
The soul of Love, Love's intellectual law:—
Hence, if we wept, it was not done in shame;
Our tears from passion and from reason came,
And, therefore, shalt thou be an honoured name!

SONNET.

ADMONITION,

(Intended more particularly for the Perusal of those who may have
happened to be enamoured of some beautiful Place of Retreat, in
the Country of the Lakes.)

Yes, there is holy pleasure in thine eye!
—The lovely Cottage in the guardian nook
Hath stirr'd thee deeply; with its own dear brook,
Its own small pasture, almost its own sky!
But covet not th' Abode—oh! do not sigh,
As many do, repining while they look,
Sighing a wish to tear from Nature's Book
This blissful leaf, with worst impiety.
Think what the home would be if it were thine,

Even thine, though few thy wants!—Roof, window, door,
The very flowers are sacred to the Poor,
The roses to the porch which they entwine:
Yea, all, that now enchants thee, from the day
On which it should be touch'd, would melt, and melt away!

SONNET.

... "*gives to airy nothing
A local habitation and a name.*"

Though narrow be that Old Man's cares, and near
The poor Old Man is greater than he seems:
For he hath waking empire, wide as dreams;
An ample sovereignty of eye and ear.
Rich are his walks with supernatural chear;
The region of his inner spirit teems
With vital sounds, and monitory gleams
Of high astonishment and pleasing fear.
He the seven birds hath seen that never part,
Seen the SEVEN WHISTLERS in their nightly rounds,
And counted them: and oftentimes will start—
For overhead are sweeping GABRIEL'S HOUNDS,
Doom'd, with their impious Lord, the flying Hart
To chase for ever, on aerial grounds.

SONNET.

A PROPHECY.
Feb. 1807.

    High deeds, O Germans, are to come from you!
Thus in your Books the record shall be found,
"A Watchword was pronounced, a potent sound,
ARMINIUS!—all the people quaked like dew
Stirr'd by the breeze—they rose, a Nation, true,
True to itself—the mighty Germany,
She of the Danube and the Northern sea,
She rose,—and off at once the yoke she threw.
All power was given her in the dreadful trance—
Those new-born Kings she wither'd like a flame."
—Woe to them all! but heaviest woe and shame
To that Bavarian, who did first advance
His banner in accursed league with France,
First open Traitor to her sacred name!

SONNET,
TO THOMAS CLARKSON,
On the final passing of the Bill for the Abolition of the Slave
Trade, March, 1807.

Clarkson! it was an obstinate Hill to climb;
How toilsome, nay how dire it was, by Thee
Is known,—by none, perhaps, so feelingly;
But Thou, who, starting in thy fervent prime,
Didst first lead forth this pilgrimage sublime,
Hast heard the constant Voice its charge repeat,
Which, out of thy young heart's oracular seat,
First roused thee.—O true yoke-fellow of Time
With unabating effort, see, the palm
Is won, and by all Nations shall be worn!
The bloody Writing is for ever torn,
And Thou henceforth shalt have a good Man's calm,
A great Man's happiness; thy zeal shall find
Repose at length, firm Friend of human kind!

* * * * *

Once in a lonely Hamlet I sojourn'd
In which a Lady driv'n from France did dwell;
The big and lesser griefs, with which she mourn'd,
In friendship she to me would often tell.

This Lady, dwelling upon English ground,
Where she was childless, daily did repair

To a poor neighbouring Cottage; as I found,
For sake of a young Child whose home was there.

Once did I see her clasp the Child about,
And take it to herself; and I, next day, 10
Wish'd in my native tongue to fashion out
Such things as she unto this Child might say:
And thus, from what I knew, had heard, and guess'd,
My song the workings of her heart express'd.

"Dear Babe, thou Daughter of another,
One moment let me be thy Mother!
An Infant's face and looks are thine;
And sure a Mother's heart is mine:
Thy own dear Mother's far away,
At labour in the harvest-field: 20
Thy little Sister is at play;—
What warmth, what comfort would it yield
To my poor heart, if Thou wouldst be
One little hour a child to me!"

"Across the waters I am come,
And I have left a Babe at home:
A long, long way of land and sea!
Come to me—I'm no enemy:
I am the same who at thy side
Sate yesterday, and made a nest 30
For thee, sweet Baby!—thou hast tried.
Thou know'st, the pillow of my breast:
Good, good art thou; alas! to me
Far more than I can be to thee."

"Here little Darling dost thou lie;
An Infant Thou, a Mother I!
Mine wilt thou be, thou hast no fears;
Mine art thou—spite of these my tears.
Alas! before I left the spot,
My Baby and its dwelling-place; 40
The Nurse said to me, 'Tears should not
Be shed upon an Infant's face,
It was unlucky'—no, no, no;
No truth is in them who say so!"

"My own dear Little-one will sigh,
Sweet Babe! and they will let him die.
'He pines,' they'll say, 'it is his doom,
And you may see his hour is come.'
Oh! had he but thy chearful smiles,
Limbs stout as thine, and lips as gay, 50
Thy looks, thy cunning, and thy wiles,
And countenance like a summer's day,
They would have hopes of him—and then
I should behold his face again!"

"'Tis gone—forgotten—let me do
My best—there was a smile or two,
I can remember them, I see
The smiles, worth all the world to me.
Dear Baby! I must lay thee down;
Thou troublest me with strange alarms; 60
Smiles hast Thou, sweet ones of thy own;
I cannot keep thee in my arms,
For they confound me: as it is,
I have forgot those smiles of his."

"Oh! how I love thee! we will stay
Together here this one half day.
My Sister's Child, who bears my name,
From France across the Ocean came;
She with her Mother cross'd the sea;
The Babe and Mother near me dwell: 70
My Darling, she is not to me
What thou art! though I love her well:
Rest, little Stranger, rest thee here;
Never was any Child more dear!"

"—I cannot help it—ill intent
I've none, my pretty Innocent!
I weep—I know they do thee wrong,
These tears—and my poor idle tongue.
Oh what a kiss was that! my cheek
How cold it is! but thou art good; 80
Thine eyes are on me—they would speak,
I think, to help me if they could.
Blessings upon that quiet face,
My heart again is in its place!"

"While thou art mine, my little Love,
This cannot be a sorrowful grove;
Contentment, hope, and Mother's glee.
I seem to find them all in thee:
Here's grass to play with, here are flowers;
I'll call thee by my Darling's name; 90
Thou hast, I think, a look of ours,
Thy features seem to me the same;
His little Sister thou shalt be;

And, when once more my home I see,
I'll tell him many tales of Thee."

FORESIGHT.
Or the Charge of a Child to his younger Companion.

   That is work which I am rueing—
Do as Charles and I are doing!
Strawberry-blossoms, one and all,
We must spare them—here are many:
Look at it—the Flower is small,
Small and low, though fair as any:
Do not touch it! summers two
I am older, Anne, than you.

   Pull the Primrose, Sister Anne!
Pull as many as you can. 10
—Here are Daisies, take your fill;
Pansies, and the Cuckow-flower:
Of the lofty Daffodil
Make your bed, and make your bower;
Fill your lap, and fill your bosom;
Only spare the Strawberry-blossom!

   Primroses, the Spring may love them—
Summer knows but little of them:
Violets, do what they will,
Wither'd on the ground must lie; 20

Daisies will be daisies still;
Daisies they must live and die:
Fill your lap, and fill your bosom,
Only spare the Strawberry-blossom!

A COMPLAINT.

There is a change—and I am poor;
Your Love hath been, nor long ago,
A Fountain at my fond Heart's door,
Whose only business was to flow;
And flow it did; not taking heed
Of its own bounty, or my need.

What happy moments did I count!
Bless'd was I then all bliss above!
Now, for this consecrated Fount
Of murmuring, sparkling, living love,
What have I? shall I dare to tell?
A comfortless, and hidden WELL.

A Well of love—it may be deep—
I trust it is, and never dry:
What matter? if the Waters sleep
In silence and obscurity.
—Such change, and at the very door
Of my fond Heart, hath made me poor.

* * * * *

I am not One who much or oft delight
To season my fireside with personal talk,
About Friends, who live within an easy walk,
Or Neighbours, daily, weekly, in my sight:
And, for my chance-acquaintance, Ladies bright,
Sons, Mothers, Maidens withering on the stalk,
These all wear out of me, like Forms, with chalk
Painted on rich men's floors, for one feast-night.
Better than such discourse doth silence long,
Long, barren silence, square with my desire; 10
To sit without emotion, hope, or aim,
By my half-kitchen my half-parlour fire,
And listen to the flapping of the flame,
Or kettle, whispering its faint undersong.

"Yet life," you say, "is life; we have seen and see,
And with a living pleasure we describe;
And fits of sprightly malice do but bribe
The languid mind into activity.
Sound sense, and love itself, and mirth and glee,
Are foster'd by the comment and the gibe." 20
Even be it so: yet still among your tribe,
Our daily world's true Worldlings, rank not me!
Children are blest, and powerful; their world lies
More justly balanced; partly at their feet,
And part far from them:—sweetest melodies
Are those that are by distance made more sweet;
Whose mind is but the mind of his own eyes
He is a Slave; the meanest we can meet!

Wings have we, and as far as we can go
We may find pleasure: wilderness and wood, 30
Blank ocean and mere sky, support that mood
Which with the lofty sanctifies the low:
Dreams, books, are each a world; and books, we know,
Are a substantial world, both pure and good:
Round these, with tendrils strong as flesh and blood,
Our pastime and our happiness will grow.
There do I find a never-failing store
Of personal themes, and such as I love best;
Matter wherein right voluble I am:
Two will I mention, dearer than the rest; 40
The gentle Lady, married to the Moor;
And heavenly Una with her milk-white Lamb.

Nor can I not believe but that hereby
Great gains are mine: for thus I live remote
From evil-speaking; rancour, never sought,
Comes to me not; malignant truth, or lie.
Hence have I genial seasons, hence have I
Smooth passions, smooth discourse, and joyous thought:
And thus from day to day my little Boat
Rocks in its harbour, lodging peaceably. 50
Blessings be with them, and eternal praise,
Who gave us nobler loves, and nobler cares,
The Poets, who on earth have made us Heirs
Of truth and pure delight by heavenly lays!
Oh! might my name be numbered among theirs,
Then gladly would I end my mortal days.

* * * * *

Yes! full surely 'twas the Echo,
Solitary, clear, profound,
Answering to Thee, shouting Cuckoo!
Giving to thee Sound for Sound.

Whence the Voice? from air or earth?
This the Cuckoo cannot tell;
But a startling sound had birth,
As the Bird must know full well;

Like the voice through earth and sky
By the restless Cuckoo sent; 10
Like her ordinary cry,
Like—but oh how different!

Hears not also mortal Life?
Hear not we, unthinking Creatures!
Slaves of Folly, Love, or Strife,
Voices of two different Natures?

Have not We too? Yes we have
Answers, and we know not whence;
Echoes from beyond the grave,
Recogniz'd intelligence? 20

Such within ourselves we hear
Oft-times, ours though sent from far;
Listen, ponder, hold them dear;
For of God, of God they are!

TO THE SPADE OF A FRIEND, (AN AGRICULTURIST.)

Composed while we were labouring together in his Pleasure-Ground.

Spade! with which Wilkinson hath till'd his Lands,
And shap'd these pleasant walks by Emont's side,
Thou art a tool of honour in my hands;
I press thee through the yielding soil with pride.

Rare Master has it been thy lot to know;
Long hast Thou serv'd a Man to reason true;
Whose life combines the best of high and low,
The toiling many and the resting few;

Health, quiet, meekness, ardour, hope secure,
And industry of body and of mind; 10
And elegant enjoyments, that are pure
As Nature is; too pure to be refined.

Here often hast Thou heard the Poet sing
In concord with his River murmuring by;
Or in some silent field, while timid Spring
Is yet uncheer'd by other minstrelsy.

Who shall inherit Thee when Death hath laid
Low in the darksome Cell thine own dear Lord?
That Man will have a trophy, humble, Spade!
More noble than the noblest Warrior's sword. 20

If he be One that feels, with skill to part
False praise from true, or greater from the less,

Thee will he welcome to his hand and heart,
Thou monument of peaceful happiness!

With Thee he will not dread a toilsome day,
His powerful Servant, his inspiring Mate!
And, when thou art past service, worn away,
Thee a surviving soul shall consecrate.

His thrift thy uselessness will never scorn;
An *Heir-loom* in his cottage wilt thou be:— 30
High will he hang thee up, and will adorn
His rustic chimney with the last of Thee!

SONG, AT THE FEAST OF BROUGHAM CASTLE, UPON THE RESTORATION OF LORD CLIFFORD, THE SHEPHERD,
to the Estates and Honours of his Ancestors.

High in the breathless Hall the Minstrel sate.
And Emont's murmur mingled with the Song.—
The words of ancient time I thus translate,
A festal Strain that hath been silent long.

From Town to Town, from Tower to Tower,
The Red Rose is a gladsome Flower.
Her thirty years of Winter past;
The Red Rose is revived at last;

She lifts her head for endless spring,
For everlasting blossoming! 10
Both Roses flourish, Red and White.
In love and sisterly delight
The two that were at strife are blended,
And all old sorrows now are ended.—
Joy! joy to both! but most to her
Who is the Flower of Lancaster!
Behold her how She smiles to day
On this great throng, this bright array!
Fair greeting doth she send to all
From every corner of the Hall; 20
But, chiefly, from above the Board
Where sits in state our rightful Lord,
A Clifford to his own restored.

They came with banner, spear, and shield;
And it was proved in Bosworth-field.
Not long the Avenger was withstood,
Earth help'd him with the cry of blood:
St. George was for us, and the might
Of blessed Angels crown'd the right.
Loud voice the Land hath utter'd forth, 30
We loudest in the faithful North:
Our Fields rejoice, our Mountains ring,
Our Streams proclaim a welcoming;
Our Strong-abodes and Castles see
The glory of their loyalty.
How glad is Skipton at this hour
Though she is but a lonely Tower!
Silent, deserted of her best,
Without an Inmate or a Guest,

Knight, Squire, or Yeoman, Page, or Groom; 40
We have them at the Feast of Brough'm.
How glad Pendragon though the sleep
Of years be on her!—She shall reap
A taste of this great pleasure, viewing
As in a dream her own renewing.
Rejoiced is Brough, right glad I deem
Beside her little humble Stream;
And she that keepeth watch and ward
Her statelier Eden's course to guard;
They both are happy at this hour, 50
Though each is but a lonely Tower:—
But here is perfect joy and pride
For one fair House by Emont's side,
This day distinguished without peer
To see her Master and to cheer;
Him, and his Lady Mother dear.

　　Oh! it was a time forlorn
When the Fatherless was born—
Give her wings that she may fly,
Or she sees her Infant die! 60
Swords that are with slaughter wild
Hunt the Mother and the Child.
Who will take them from the light?
—Yonder is a Man in sight—
Yonder is a House—but where?
No, they must not enter there.
To the Caves, and to the Brooks,
To the Clouds of Heaven she looks;
She is speechless, but her eyes
Pray in ghostly agonies. 70

Blissful Mary, Mother mild,
Maid and Mother undefiled,
Save a Mother and her Child!

    Now Who is he that bounds with joy
On Carrock's side, a Shepherd Boy?
No thoughts hath he but thoughts that pass
Light as the wind along the grass.
Can this be He who hither came
In secret, like a smothered flame?
O'er whom such thankful tears were shed 80
For shelter, and a poor Man's bread?
God loves the Child; and God hath will'd
That those dear words should be fulfill'd,
The Lady's words, when forc'd away,
The last she to her Babe did say,
"My own, my own, thy Fellow-guest
I may not be; but rest thee, rest,
For lowly Shepherd's life is best!"

    Alas! when evil men are strong
No life is good, no pleasure long. 90
The Boy must part from Mosedale's Groves,
And leave Blencathara's rugged Coves,
And quit the Flowers that Summer brings
To Glenderamakin's lofty springs;
Must vanish, and his careless cheer
Be turned to heaviness and fear.
—Give Sir Lancelot Threlkeld praise!
Hear it, good Man, old in days!
Thou Tree of covert and of rest
For this young Bird that is distrest, 100

Among thy branches safe he lay,
And he was free to sport and play,
When Falcons were abroad for prey.

   A recreant Harp, that sings of fear
And heaviness in Clifford's ear!
I said, when evil Men are strong,
No life is good, no pleasure long,
A weak and cowardly untruth!
Our Clifford was a happy Youth,
And thankful through a weary time, 110
That brought him up to manhood's prime.
—Again he wanders forth at will,
And tends a Flock from hill to hill:
His garb is humble; ne'er was seen
Such garb with such a noble mien;
Among the Shepherd-grooms no Mate
Hath he, a Child of strength and state!
Yet lacks not friends for solemn glee,
And a chearful company,
That learn'd of him submissive ways; 120
And comforted his private days.
To his side the Fallow-deer
Came, and rested without fear;
The Eagle, Lord of land and sea,
Stoop'd down to pay him fealty;
And both the undying Fish that swim
Through Bowscale-Tarn did wait on him,
The pair were Servants of his eye
In their immortality,
They moved about in open sight, 130
To and fro, for his delight.

He knew the Rocks which Angels haunt
On the Mountains visitant;
He hath kenn'd them taking wing:
And the Caves where Faeries sing
He hath entered; and been told
By Voices how Men liv'd of old.
Among the Heavens his eye can see
Face of thing that is to be;
And, if Men report him right, 140
He can whisper words of might.
—Now another day is come,
Fitter hope, and nobler doom:
He hath thrown aside his Crook,
And hath buried deep his Book;
Armour rusting in his Halls
On the blood of Clifford calls;—

"Quell the Scot," exclaims the Lance,
"Bear me to the heart of France,
Is the longing of the Shield— 150
Tell thy name, thou trembling Field;
Field of death, where'er thou be,
Groan thou with our victory!
Happy day, and mighty hour,
When our Shepherd, in his power,
Mail'd and hors'd, with lance and sword,
To his Ancestors restored,
Like a reappearing Star,
Like a glory from afar,
First shall head the Flock of War!" 160

Alas! the fervent Harper did not know
That for a tranquil Soul the Lay was framed,
Who, long compell'd in humble walks to go,
Was softened into feeling, sooth'd, and tamed.
Love had he found in huts where poor Men lie,
His daily Teachers had been Woods and Rills,
The silence that is in the starry sky,
The sleep that is among the lonely hills.

In him the savage Virtue of the Race,
Revenge, and all ferocious thoughts were dead: 170
Nor did he change; but kept in lofty place
The wisdom which adversity had bred.

Glad were the Vales, and every cottage hearth;
The Shepherd Lord was honour'd more and more:
And, ages after he was laid in earth,
"The Good Lord Clifford" was the name he bore.

LINES,

Composed at GRASMERE, during a walk, one Evening, after
a stormy day, the Author having just read in a Newspaper
that the dissolution of MR. FOX was hourly expected.

Loud is the Vale! the Voice is up
With which she speaks when storms are gone,
A mighty Unison of streams!
Of all her Voices, One!

Loud is the Vale;—this inland Depth
In peace is roaring like the Sea;
Yon Star upon the mountain-top
Is listening quietly.

Sad was I, ev'n to pain depress'd,
Importunate and heavy load! 10
The Comforter hath found me here,
Upon this lonely road;

And many thousands now are sad,
Wait the fulfilment of their fear;
For He must die who is their Stay,
Their Glory disappear.

A Power is passing from the earth
To breathless Nature's dark abyss;
But when the Mighty pass away
What is it more than this, 20

That Man, who is from God sent forth,
Doth yet again to God return?—
Such ebb and flow must ever be,
Then wherefore should we mourn?

ELEGIAC STANZAS,

Suggested by a Picture of PEELE CASTLE, in a Storm, *painted* BY SIR GEORGE BEAUMONT.

I was thy Neighbour once, thou rugged Pile!
Four summer weeks I dwelt in sight of thee:
I saw thee every day; and all the while
Thy Form was sleeping on a glassy sea.

So pure the sky, so quiet was the air!
So like, so very like, was day to day!
Whene'er I look'd, thy Image still was there;
It trembled, but it never pass'd away.

How perfect was the calm! it seem'd no sleep;
No mood, which season takes away, or brings: 10
I could have fancied that the mighty Deep
Was even the gentlest of all gentle Things.

Ah! THEN, if mine had been the Painter's hand,
To express what then I saw; and add the gleam,
The light that never was, on sea or land,
The consecration, and the Poet's dream;

I would have planted thee, thou hoary Pile!
Amid a world how different from this!
Beside a sea that could not cease to smile;
On tranquil land, beneath a sky of bliss: 20

Thou shouldst have seem'd a treasure-house, a mine
Of peaceful years; a chronicle of heaven:—

Of all the sunbeams that did ever shine
The very sweetest had to thee been given.

    A Picture had it been of lasting ease,
Elysian quiet, without toil or strife;
No motion but the moving tide, a breeze,
Or merely silent Nature's breathing life.

    Such, in the fond delusion of my heart,
Such Picture would I at that time have made: 30
And seen the soul of truth in every part;
A faith, a trust, that could not be betray'd.

    So once it would have been,—'tis so no more;
I have submitted to a new controul:
A power is gone, which nothing can restore;
A deep distress hath humaniz'd my Soul.

    Not for a moment could I now behold
A smiling sea and be what I have been:
The feeling of my loss will ne'er be old;
This, which I know, I speak with mind serene. 40

    Then, Beaumont, Friend! who would have been the Friend,
If he had lived, of Him whom I deplore,
This Work of thine I blame not, but commend;
This sea in anger, and that dismal shore.

    Oh 'tis a passionate Work!—yet wise and well;
Well chosen is the spirit that is here;
That Hulk which labours in the deadly swell,
This rueful sky, this pageantry of fear!

And this huge Castle, standing here sublime,
I love to see the look with which it braves, 50
Cased in the unfeeling armour of old time,
The light'ning, the fierce wind, and trampling waves.

Farewell, farewell the Heart that lives alone,
Hous'd in a dream, at distance from the Kind!
Such happiness, wherever it be known,
Is to be pitied; for 'tis surely blind.

But welcome fortitude, and patient chear,
And frequent sights of what is to be born!
Such sights, or worse, as are before me here.—
Not without hope we suffer and we mourn. 60

ODE.

Paulo majora canamus.

ODE.

There was a time when meadow, grove, and stream,
The earth, and every common sight,
    To me did seem
    Apparell'd in celestial light,
The glory and the freshness of a dream.
It is not now as it has been of yore;—
    Turn wheresoe'er I may,

By night or day,
The things which I have seen I now can see no more.

    The Rainbow comes and goes, 10
    And lovely is the Rose,
    The Moon doth with delight
Look round her when the heavens are bare;
    Waters on a starry night
    Are beautiful and fair;
    The sunshine is a glorious birth;
    But yet I know, where'er I go,
That there hath pass'd away a glory from the earth.

  Now, while the Birds thus sing a joyous song,
    And while the young Lambs bound 20
    As to the tabor's sound,
To me alone there came a thought of grief:
A timely utterance gave that thought relief,
    And I again am strong.
The Cataracts blow their trumpets from the steep,
No more shall grief of mine the season wrong;
I hear the Echoes through the mountains throng,
The Winds come to me from the fields of sleep,

    And all the earth is gay,
    Land and sea 30
  Give themselves up to jollity,
    And with the heart of May
Doth every Beast keep holiday,
    Thou Child of Joy
Shout round me, let me hear thy shouts, thou happy Shepherd
Boy!

Ye blessed Creatures, I have heard the call
    Ye to each other make; I see
The heavens laugh with you in your jubilee;
    My heart is at your festival,
        My head hath its coronal, 40
The fullness of your bliss, I feel—I feel it all.
        Oh evil day! if I were sullen
        While the Earth herself is adorning,
            This sweet May-morning,
        And the Children are pulling,
            On every side,
        In a thousand vallies far and wide,
        Fresh flowers; while the sun shines warm,
And the Babe leaps up on his mother's arm:—
        I hear, I hear, with joy I hear! 50
—But there's a Tree, of many one,
A single Field which I have look'd upon,
Both of them speak of something that is gone:
        The Pansy at my feet
        Doth the same tale repeat:
Whither is fled the visionary gleam?
Where is it now, the glory and the dream?

    Our birth is but a sleep and a forgetting:
The Soul that rises with us, our life's Star,
        Hath had elsewhere its setting, 60
            And cometh from afar:
        Not in entire forgetfulness,
        And not in utter nakedness,
But trailing clouds of glory do we come
        From God, who is our home;
Heaven lies about us in our infancy!

Shades of the prison-house begin to close
     Upon the growing Boy,
But He beholds the light, and whence it flows,
     He sees it in his joy; 70
The Youth, who daily farther from the East
  Must travel, still is Nature's Priest,
    And by the vision splendid
    Is on his way attended;
At length the Man perceives it die away,
And fade into the light of common day.

  Earth fills her lap with pleasures of her own;
Yearnings she hath in her own natural kind,
And, even with something of a Mother's mind,
    And no unworthy aim, 80
  The homely Nurse doth all she can
To make her Foster-child, her Inmate Man,
   Forget the glories he hath known,
And that imperial palace whence he came.

  Behold the Child among his new-born blisses,
A four year's Darling of a pigmy size!
See, where mid work of his own hand he lies,
Fretted by sallies of his Mother's kisses,
With light upon him from his Father's eyes!
See, at his feet, some little plan or chart, 90
Some fragment from his dream of human life,
Shap'd by himself with newly-learned art;
   A wedding or a festival,
   A mourning or a funeral;
    And this hath now his heart,
    And unto this he frames his song:

Then will he fit his tongue
To dialogues of business, love, or strife;

But it will not be long
Ere this be thrown aside, 100
And with new joy and pride
The little Actor cons another part,
Filling from time to time his "humourous stage"
With all the Persons, down to palsied Age,
That Life brings with her in her Equipage;
As if his whole vocation
Were endless imitation.

Thou, whose exterior semblance doth belie
Thy Soul's immensity;
Thou best Philosopher, who yet dost keep 110
Thy heritage, thou Eye among the blind,
That, deaf and silent, read'st the eternal deep,
Haunted for ever by the eternal mind,—
Mighty Prophet! Seer blest!
On whom those truths do rest,
Which we are toiling all our lives to find;
Thou, over whom thy Immortality

Broods like the Day, a Master o'er a Slave,
A Presence which is not to be put by;
To whom the grave 120
Is but a lonely bed without the sense or sight
Of day or the warm light,
A place of thought where we in waiting lie;
Thou little Child, yet glorious in the might
Of untam'd pleasures, on thy Being's height,
Why with such earnest pains dost thou provoke

The Years to bring the inevitable yoke,
Thus blindly with thy blessedness at strife?
Full soon thy Soul shall have her earthly freight,
And custom lie upon thee with a weight, 130
Heavy as frost, and deep almost as life!

O joy! that in our embers
Is something that doth live,
That nature yet remembers
What was so fugitive!

The thought of our past years in me doth breed
Perpetual benedictions: not indeed
For that which is most worthy to be blest;
Delight and liberty, the simple creed
Of Childhood, whether fluttering or at rest, 140
With new-born hope for ever in his breast:—
Not for these I raise
The song of thanks and praise;
But for those obstinate questionings
Of sense and outward things,
Fallings from us, vanishings;
Blank misgivings of a Creature
Moving about in worlds not realiz'd,
High instincts, before which our mortal Nature
Did tremble like a guilty Thing surpriz'd: 150
But for those first affections,
Those shadowy recollections,
Which, be they what they may,
Are yet the fountain light of all our day,
Are yet a master light of all our seeing;
Uphold us, cherish us, and make

Our noisy years seem moments in the being
Of the eternal Silence: truths that wake,
      To perish never;
Which neither listlessness, nor mad endeavour, 160
      Nor Man nor Boy,
Nor all that is at enmity with joy,
Can utterly abolish or destroy!
  Hence, in a season of calm weather,
    Though inland far we be,
Our Souls have sight of that immortal sea
      Which brought us hither,
      Can in a moment travel thither,
And see the Children sport upon the shore,
And hear the mighty waters rolling evermore. 170

  Then, sing ye Birds, sing, sing a joyous song!
    And let the young Lambs bound
    As to the tabor's sound!
  We in thought will join your throng,
    Ye that pipe and ye that play,
    Ye that through your hearts to day
    Feel the gladness of the May!
What though the radiance which was once so bright
Be now for ever taken from my sight,
  Though nothing can bring back the hour 180
Of splendour in the grass, of glory in the flower;
    We will grieve not, rather find
    Strength in what remains behind,
    In the primal sympathy
    Which having been must ever be,
    In the soothing thoughts that spring
    Out of human suffering,

In the faith that looks through death,
In years that bring the philosophic mind.

And oh ye Fountains, Meadows, Hills, and Groves, 190
Think not of any severing of our loves!
Yet in my heart of hearts I feel your might;
I only have relinquish'd one delight
To live beneath your more habitual sway.
I love the Brooks which down their channels fret,
Even more than when I tripp'd lightly as they;
The innocent brightness of a new-born Day
　　　Is lovely yet;
The Clouds that gather round the setting sun
Do take a sober colouring from an eye 200
That hath kept watch o'er man's mortality;
Another race hath been, and other palms are won.
Thanks to the human heart by which we live,
Thanks to its tenderness, its joys, and fears,
To me the meanest flower that blows can give
Thoughts that do often lie too deep for tears.

NOTES TO THE SECOND VOLUME.

NOTES.

NOTE I.

PAGE 8; —"And wondrous length and strength of arm." The people of the neighbourhood of Loch Ketterine, in order to prove the extraordinary length of their Hero's arm, tell you that "he could garter his Tartan Stockings below the knee when standing upright." According to their account he was a tremendous Swordsman; after having sought all occasions of proving his prowess, he was never conquered but once, and this not till he was an Old Man.

NOTE II.

PAGE 93.—*The solitary Reaper*. This Poem was suggested by a beautiful sentence in a MS Tour in Scotland written by a Friend, the last line being taken from it *verbatim*.

NOTE III.

PAGE 120.—THE BLIND HIGHLAND BOY. The incident upon which this Poem is founded was related to me by an eye witness.

NOTE IV.

PAGE 142; line 10.—"Seen the Seven Whistlers, &c." Both these superstitions are prevalent in the midland Counties of England: that of "Gabriel's Hounds" appears to be very general over Europe; being the same as the one upon which the German Poet, Burger, has founded his Ballad of the Wild Huntsman.

NOTE V.

PAGE 154.—*Song, at the Feast of Brougham Castle.* Henry Lord Clifford, &c. &c., who is the subject of this Poem, was the son of John, Lord Clifford, who was slain at Towton Field, which John, Lord Clifford, as is known to the Reader of English History, was the person who after the battle of Wakefield slew, in the pursuit, the young Earl of Rutland, Son of the Duke of York who had fallen in the battle, "in part of revenge" (say the Authors of the History of Cumberland and Westmorland); "for the Earl's Father had slain his." A deed which worthily blemished the author (saith Speed); But who, as he adds, "dare promise any thing temperate of himself in the heat of martial fury? chiefly, when it was resolved not to leave any branch of the York line standing; for so one maketh this Lord to speak." This, no doubt, I would observe by the bye, was an action sufficiently in the vindictive spirit of the times, and yet not altogether so bad as represented; for the Earl was no child, as some writers would have him, but able to bear arms, being sixteen or seventeen years of age, as is evident from this (say the Memoirs of the Countess of Pembroke, who was laudably anxious to wipe away, as far as could be, this stigma from the illustrious name to which she was born); that he was the next Child to King Edward the Fourth, which his mother had by Richard Duke of York, and that King was then eighteen years of age: and for the small distance betwixt her Children, see Austin Vincent in his book of Nobility, page 622, where he writes of them all. It may further be observed, that Lord Clifford, who was then himself only twenty-five years of age, had been a leading Man and Commander, two or three years together in the Army of Lancaster, before this time;

and, therefore, would be less likely to think that the Earl of Rutland might be entitled to mercy from his youth.—But, independent of this act, at best a cruel and savage one, the Family of Clifford had done enough to draw upon them the vehement hatred of the House of York: so that after the Battle of Towton there was no hope for them but in flight and concealment. Henry, the subject of the Poem, was deprived of his estate and honours during the space of twenty-four years; all which time he lived as a shepherd in Yorkshire, or in Cumberland, where the estate of his Father-in-law (Sir Lancelot Threlkeld) lay. He was restored to his estate and honours in the first year of Henry the Seventh. It is recorded that, "when called to parliament, he behaved nobly and wisely; but otherwise came seldom to London or the Court; and rather delighted to live in the country, where he repaired several of his Castles, which had gone to decay during the late troubles." Thus far is chiefly collected from Nicholson and Burn; and I can add, from my own knowledge, that there is a tradition current in the village of Threlkeld and its neighbourhood, his principal retreat, that, in the course of his shepherd life, he had acquired great astronomical knowledge. I cannot conclude this note without adding a word upon the subject of those numerous and noble feudal Edifices, spoken of in the Poem, the ruins of some of which are, at this day, so great an ornament to that interesting country. The Cliffords had always been distinguished for an honorable pride in these Castles; and we have seen that after the wars of York and Lancaster they were rebuilt; in the civil Wars of Charles the First, they were again laid waste, and again restored almost to their former magnificence by the celebrated Lady Anne Clifford, Countess of Pembroke, &c. &c. Not more than 25 years after this was done, when the Estates of Clifford had passed into the family of Tufton, three of these Castles, namely Brough, Brougham, and Pendragon, were demolished, and the timber and other materials sold by Thomas Earl of Thanet. We will hope that, when this order was issued, the

Earl had not consulted the text of Isaiah, 58th Chap. 12th Verse, to which the inscription placed over the gate of Pendragon Castle, by the Countess of Pembroke (I believe his Grandmother) at the time she repaired that structure, refers the reader. "*And they that shall be of thee shall build the old waste places; thou shalt raise up the foundations of many generations, and thou shalt be called the repairer of the breach, the restorer of paths to dwell in.*" The Earl of Thanet, the present possessor of the Estates, with a due respect for the memory of his ancestors, and a proper sense of the value and beauty of these remains of antiquity, has (I am told) given orders that they shall be preserved from all depredations.

NOTE VI.

PAGE 155;—"Earth helped him with the cry of blood." This line is from The Battle of Bosworth Field by Sir John Beaumont (Brother to the Dramatist), whose poems are written with so much spirit, elegance, and harmony, that it is supposed, as the Book is very scarce, a new edition of it would be acceptable to Scholars and Men of taste, and, accordingly, it is in contemplation to give one.

NOTE VII.

PAGE 158.—

"And both the undying Fish that swim
Through Bowscale-Tarn," &c.

It is imagined by the people of the Country that there are two immortal Fish, Inhabitants of this Tarn, which lies in the mountains not far from Threlkeld.—Blencathara, mentioned before, is the old and proper name of the mountain vulgarly called Saddle-back.

NOTE VIII.

PAGE 159.—

> "Armour rusting in his Halls
> On the blood of Clifford calls."

The martial character of the Cliffords is well known to the readers of English History; but it may not be improper here to say, by way of comment on these lines and what follows, that, besides several others who perished in the same manner, the four immediate Progenitors of the person in whose hearing this is supposed to be spoken, all died in the Field.

NOTE IX.

PAGE 161.—

> "Importunate and heavy load!"

* * * * *

'Importuna e grave salma.' —MICHAEL ANGELO.

DETAILED HISTORICAL CONTEXT
POEMS IN TWO VOLUMES

INTRODUCTION

The nineteenth century was a fascinating and crucial formative period in Western literature since it served as the primary context for the future evolution and emergence of modern literary traditions and styles as we know them. For instance, additional research reveals that the Romantic, Symbolist, and Realist movements, as well as numerous social and economic situations that dominated the twentieth century, had their origins and ancestors in the nineteenth century.

MOVEMENTS AND LITERATURE

ROMANTICISM

The Romantic movement, with its contrastive focus on emotion and the irrational, offered a fresh perspective in the 19th century. In contrast, the 18th century was thought of as the age of reason, logic, and intellect. Romanticism, which arose from the German Sturm und Drang ("Stress and Storm") movement of the late 18th century and whose renowned members included Goethe and Friedrich Schiller, was distinguished by a stress on the individual, the subjective, the mystical, emotional, and inner life. It had a big influence on music, art, literature, and even architecture.

- *Rousseau*

Swiss philosopher Jean-Jacques Rousseau of the 18th century had an effect on the Preromantic and Romantic movements, as well as the Age of Enlightenment and some parts of the French Revolution, with his stress on the individual and the necessity of inspiration.

- *Early Romantic poets*

The Lyrical Ballads collection of poetry by the Romantic English poets William Wordsworth and Samuel Taylor Coleridge, published in 1798, is regarded as the precursor to this trend in the late 18th and early 19th centuries. Pushkin's poetry in Russia, Ugo Foscolo's and Giacomo Leopardi's in Italy, José de Espronceda's in Spain, and Giacomo Leopardi's in France demonstrate how the Romantic poetry movement spread throughout Europe and beyond.

- *American Romanticism*

James Fenimore Cooper's historical adventure novels, Edgar Allan Poe's supernatural and mystical writings, Walt Whitman's poetry, and Emerson and Henry David Thoreau's Transcendentalist scriptures are just a few instances of the Romantic movement's effect and growth in America.

- *Second Generation Romantic poets*

To uncover the "truth" of things, the Romantics appealed to people's emotions, which were anchored in and exemplified by interaction with nature and the primordial self, rather than intellectual examination. Excellent examples of these points of view may be found in the works of the second generation Romantic poets John Keats, Lord Byron, and Percy Bysshe Shelley.

POST ROMANTICISM

- *Parnassianism*

The works of French poets Théophile Gautier and Charles Baudelaire are examples of Parnassianism, which may be regarded of as an extension of early Romantic perspectives with its emphasis on aesthetics and the concept of art for art's sake. Schopenhauer's philosophical viewpoints also had an effect. Devotees aimed to treat their exotic and old topics of attraction in a more controlled, formal manner, moving from the Romantic movement's excess emotion and sentimentality.

- *Impressionism and Symbolism*

Claude Monet and other Paris-based painters contributed to the development of impressionism, which was initially evident in painting and subsequently in music in France towards the end of the nineteenth century. Impressionism was a painting movement that sought to depict the visual world as faithfully as possible utilising the varying qualities of light and colour as perceived and experienced by humans.

Symbolism may be defined as a shift away from naturalism and realism and towards a harsher, more truthful picture of the world, with an emphasis on the ordinary over the spectacular. The goal of symbolist poetry, as practised by poets like Gustave Kahn and Ezra Pound, was to "evoke" rather than "depict" or "describe" through the use of imagery.

THE GOTHIC NOVEL

This was a popular subgenre of European Romantic literature beginning in the late 18th century with novels like Horace Walpole's Castle of Otranto (1765) and Ann Radcliffe's Mysteries of Udolpho. It was referred to be "gothic" because early works in this genre usually used Gothic architecture as their backdrop and setting. The idea that the characters' present-day lives are plagued by their pasts set it distinct from previous supernatural or ghost stories. Famous and well-liked 19th-century gothic novels include Dracula by Bram Stoker, The Strange Case of Dr. Jekyll and Mr. Hyde by Robert Louis Stevenson, Wuthering Heights by Emily Bronte, Frankenstein by Mark Shelley, Bride of Lammermoor by Walter Scott, The Devil's Elixirs by E.T.A. Hoffmann, and The Devil's Elixirs by E.T.A. The influence of the gothic tradition may also be seen in other well-known Victorian books like Bleak House and Great Expectations by Charles Dickens.

POPULAR PHILOSOPHY

-   *German Idealism*

Members of this school of thought included Johann Gottlieb Fichte, who developed Kantian metaphysics and argued for a self that is a "self-producing and changing process," Georg Wilhelm Friedrich Hegel, whose writings emphasised the significance of the historical thinking process in which the spirit conceives of itself, and Arthur Schopenhauer, who, in contrast to Hegel, argued for a return to Kantian transcendentalism.

- *Marxism*

A school of thought developed by Karl Marx and Friedrich Engels. Their Communist Manifesto (1848), which asserted that capitalism will inevitably self-destruct and be replaced by socialism and finally communism, laid the groundwork for the modern communist movement.

- *Positivism*

August Comte's empiricist philosophical theory argued that genuine knowledge can be seen to be true by definition or positive—that is, an a posteriori fact determined by reason and logic from sensory experience, as opposed to instinct or theology.

- *Social Darwinism*

Social Darwinism attempts to apply biological concepts of natural selection and the survival of the fittest, such as those developed and discussed in Charles Darwin's On the Origin of Species. Supporters included Francis Galton, who maintained that mental qualities, like physical ability, were inherited and that over-breeding by "less fit" members of society should be discouraged. Herbert Spencer, whose book The Social Organism (1860) views society as a living creature that evolves and develops in the same way, and Francis Spencer were also supporters.

SOCIAL, ECONOMIC AND POLITICAL IMPACTS

- *The Industrial Revolution*

The Industrial Revolution, which occurred between the late 18th century and between 1820 and 1840, was a period of great social, political, and economic uprisings and change that involved the difficult transition from largely manual production methods to mechanical manufacturing methods, particularly in the fields of textiles, steam power, iron making, and the invention of machine tools. Prior to industrialization, agriculture had formed the backbone of the European economy. At the same time, fundamental political, scientific, and religious beliefs were being completely dismantled.

As a result of this mechanisation, a considerable number of people moved from rural villages to urban regions, resulting in a major rise in population and the formation of new, bigger cities. New technology paved the door for factories, a horrifying and dehumanising kind of employment, including child exploitation, and a capitalist way of life. Due to cities' incapacity to absorb the rapidly rising population, there were overcrowded slums and terribly deplorable living conditions, as chronicled in publications such as Friedrich Engels' The Condition of the Working Class in England, published in 1844.

Elizabeth Barrett Browning's The Cry of the Children, Thomas Hardy's Tess of the D'Urbervilles, and works by author and philosopher Thomas Carlyle all foresaw the danger these inhumane practises and the profit-driven, materialistic ideals of what Carlyle referred to as the "mechanical age" in his novels Hard Times and Oliver Twist.

- *Science and influential Non-Fiction works*

The Victorians' ambition to comprehend and categorise the natural world played an important part in the development of scientific theory and understanding during the nineteenth century. Charles Darwin's works, such as the well-known On the Origin of Species (1859), would have a dramatic and far-reaching effect because of their innovative theory of evolution, which contradicted many of the time's established assumptions and religious beliefs.

The French Revolution: A History, published in 1837, and On Heroes, Hero-Worship, and the Heroic in History, published in 1841, are two additional notable non-fiction publications from the time that influenced political thinking in the mid-nineteenth century.

KEY HISTORICAL EVENTS

- *The Acts of Union and Treaty of Amiens*

Following the French Revolution and the Irish Rebellion in the late 18th century, which ushered in times of unpredictability and instability, the Acts of Union, which combined Britain and Ireland to form the combined Kingdom, were passed in 1800.

The Treaty of Amiens, which also promised to resolve the conflicts between France and the UK, put an end to the Second Coalition French Revolutionary War. However, the impact was very short-lived, as the Napoleonic Wars started in just three years.

- *US expansion*

With their freshly obtained independence, the United States decided to double their size and expand their dominance over the Mississippi River by acquiring the property known as the Louisiana Purchase in 1803. Native Americans occupy a large chunk of the territory, which was purchased from the French First Republic for $15 million.

- *Napoleonic Wars*

Napoleon conquered the Russian and Austrian armies in 1805, but his plans to invade England were thwarted when Admiral Nelson soundly defeated the French and Spanish armies at the Battle of Trafalgar, solidifying the nation's dominion over the oceans.

During the Russian invasion, the French army sustained tremendous losses—up to 380,000 soldiers died—and Napoleon's prior image as an unstoppable leader was destroyed. The French king lost the War of the Sixth Coalition in 1814, which led to his resignation and exile to Elba.

- *British and Russian empire expansion*

Following France's defeat, the British and Russian empires came to prominence as the world's two greatest powers, with Russia expanding its sphere of influence to include Central Asia and the Caucasus and Britain expanding its overseas holdings in Canada, Australia, South Africa, and Africa. The British East India Company was liquidated as a result of the Indian insurrection of 1857, a broad insurrection against colonial domination. Later, the British Raj was established, with direct government by the British Crown.

- *Opium wars*

By the middle of the nineteenth century, China had severe opium problems due to the opening of commerce with the West and the illicit traffic in the drug organised by British businesspeople eager to make money at trade ports. On the basis of free trade principles, Britain fought the emperor's attempt to ban its sale, resulting in the First Opium War and the Treaty of Nanking in 1842, which allowed the drug trade to continue and resulted in the British gaining control of Hong Kong.

The Taiping Rebellion of 1856 provided a violent background for the second Opium War, which saw the French and British join troops. The Qing dynasty was overthrown by the early 19th century as a result of the 1860 Convention of Peking, which legalised the opium trade and required the surrender of further areas.

- *The 1848 Revolutions*

The 1848 Revolutions, also known as the Springtime of the Nations, were a series of political upheavals that occurred almost simultaneously throughout Europe and the rest of the world in 1848. The main goals of these revolutions were to overthrow the existing monarchy and install free country governments.

Nationalists in Italy organised uprisings in Sicily and the Italian peninsula republics in an attempt to establish a liberal government and break free from Austrian domination. The February Revolution in France took place in Paris following the suppression of the campagne des banquets, a bloody uprising against the monarchy that resulted in the overthrow of King Louis Philippe. Numerous other countries, including Germany, Denmark, Hungary, Galicia, Sweden, and Switzerland, also had uprisings against the Habsburg Monarchy.

- *Abolitionism and the end of slavery*

The Atlantic slave trade was prohibited in the United States in 1808, and the Slavery Abolition Act, passed in 1833, prohibited slavery across the British Empire. Abolitionism triumphed throughout the 19th century. Abolitionism remained in the United States up to the end of the Civil War in 1865, which prompted the Thirteenth Amendment to the Constitution, which effectively outlawed slavery there.

- *Women's Suffrage movement*

With the Seneca Falls Convention in the United States and the National Women's Rights Convention in 1850, the demand for universal women's suffrage became stronger and louder in the 1840s. Both Sarah Grimké's The

Equality of the Sexes and the Condition of Women and Margaret Fuller's influential American feminist book Woman in the Nineteenth Century were published in 1839.

A protracted and tenacious campaign was launched in favour of a constitutional amendment on women's rights and for suffrage in every state following the early 1870s' unsuccessful attempts by suffragists to get the right to vote. Wyoming was the first state to provide women the right to vote in 1869. Emmeline Pankhurst joined and helped lead the UK suffrage campaign in 1880.